OFFICIAL SECRET

"Clutty" and some of his "toys," which were to become known as invaluable escape-aids for British prisoners-of-war.

OFFICIAL SECRET

THE REMARKABLE STORY OF ESCAPE AIDS –
THEIR INVENTION, PRODUCTION –
AND THE SEQUEL

CLAYTON HUTTON

CROWN PUBLISHERS, INC. · NEW YORK

X
09691

Third Printing, March, 1962

Contents

Illustrations

'This officer is eccentric. He cannot be expected to comply with ordinary service discipline, but he is far too valuable for his services to be lost to this department.'

Extract from letter sent by the author's
C.O. to a Provost Marshal.

OFFICIAL SECRET

1 Room 424

Three tired dahlias, drooping despondently in a jam pot on the window ledge, provided the only splash of colour in the dark and gloomy entrance hall. A trio of ancient commissionaires were moving leisurely amongst the score or so of dark-suited civilians who, like myself, were waiting to be interviewed. I wondered idly how many of them had also ascended the imposing flight of steps at the front of the building, only to be told to 'go round to the back' by a formidable fellow whose top hat and faded campaign ribbons instantly discouraged would-be gate-crashers.

I sat down at a table covered in green baize, and silently cursing the spluttering pen provided, wrote down a résumé of my business on a buff form with a surface almost as porous as blotting-paper. This was whisked away and I was left to meditate on the circumstances that had brought me to the War Office in the last week of September, 1939 . . .

During World War I, after serving in the Yeomanry and the Yorkshire Regiment, I had been a pilot in the Royal Flying Corps, so as soon as I realized that another war with Germany was inevitable, I applied to join the Royal Air Force. When I eventually discovered that my services were not wanted by the RAF, I decided to try the Army. I wrote several times to the War Office, drawing attention to my 1914–18 record and stressing the fact that I was willing to serve in no matter what capacity, but all my appeals were ignored. I then took recourse to telegrams. Working on the fairly safe assumption that they would galvanize the recipients into action, I despatched seventeen impressively lengthy wires in one week, addressing them to various departments and so wording them that they could not possibly be pushed into a 'Pending' tray and discreetly forgotten.

My unorthodox approach proved immediately successful. After six negative replies, I received an invitation to present myself at the War Office for an appointment with a Major J. H. Russell. There had been no indication as to the probable nature of the duties I might be called upon to perform, but I knew I was bound for the Intelligence branch, so I had been more than satisfied. My claim for consideration as a potential Intelligence Officer had been based on a varied and colourful life, during which I had acquired a grounding in and intimate knowledge of journalism in all its multifarious aspects, of advertising and publicity, and of the motion picture industry both in Great Britain and in America. Oddly enough, it was to be a random recollection of a boyhood experience that was ultimately to convince those in authority that I possessed the peculiar qualities they were seeking.

At this stage in my reflections I was invited to follow one of the superannuated commissionaires down one of the long corridors that radiated from the hall. We passed old men and young girls, all carrying steaming cups of tea on cheap japanned trays, and finally I was ushered into a small dimly-lit room in which no fewer than nine officers were miraculously accommodated. In an atmosphere heavy with cigarette smoke they sat, almost shoulder to shoulder, behind rough wooden tables piled high with dusty files and papers of every description. Some were bellowing vociferously into telephones; others were scribbling industriously; one – a major, distinguished-looking, grey-haired, with penetrating eyes and an indefinable charm of manner – was watching me amusedly. As I moved, rather hesitantly, towards the table, he rose and gave me an encouraging hand-shake.

'Clayton Hutton,' he stated rather than asked. 'I read your telegram. As a matter of fact, I read half a dozen others, too, sent on to me from various departments.' He gestured towards a chair pushed under the table opposite him. 'But sit down and have a cigarette. My name is Russell, by the way. Came here straight from the Temple and am still feeling my way around. My job, apparently, is to fit square pegs into square holes. Anyway, tell me all about yourself.'

Delighted by this informal approach, I closed my ears to the surrounding hubbub and talked to him through a blue haze of tobacco smoke.

'I started off by wanting to go on the stage,' I began, 'but my mother's opposition turned me towards journalism. I learned the whole business under Lord Northcliffe, and when he died in 1922, I had a long spell with the *Daily Chronicle*. Then I quit journalism to become a publicity director in the film industry. I suppose my real speciality is thinking up new ideas and then putting them across.'

Major Russell eyed me speculatively. 'Have you always been interested in show business, Mr Hutton?'

'All my life,' I admitted. 'Magicians, illusionists, escapologists in particular – they all fascinate me. I expect it goes back to the night I tried to outwit Houdini at the Birmingham "Empire". I've got a copy of the original challenge in my wallet. I remember how —'

'Let me see it,' Major Russell broke in surprisingly.

Rather taken aback by this unexpected request, I fished a folded sheet of paper from my wallet, smoothed it out and laid it on the desk. Major Russell leaned forward to study its unequivocal message, nodding to himself at intervals, as though what he was reading there served to con-

firm opinions previously formed. From where I was sitting
the words were upside-down, but I knew them by heart.

CHALLENGE

To Mr Harry Houdini
The Birmingham Empire
BIRMINGHAM

April 29th, 1913.

Dear Sir,

When you were previously in Birmingham,
you escaped from a packing-case.

As the case was delivered two days ahead, you
had ample time to tamper with it.

In order to eliminate such a possibility, will you
accept the challenge permitting us to bring to the
'Empire' timber, battens, 2½" nails, and in full view
of the audience construct a strong heavy box, you to
enter immediately, we to nail down the lid, securely
rope up the box, and defy you to escape without
demolishing same.

Yours truly,

Sgd.

EDWARD WITHERS, 26 Coventry Road
BENJAMIN WITHERS, 52 Hunton Road, Gravelly Hill
FRED LEES, 23 Craddock Road, Saltley
CLAYTON HUTTON, Washwood Heath, Birmingham

(Employees of W. J. CLAYTON LTD, Timber
   Merchants, Park Saw Mills, Birmingham)

The above *CHALLENGE has been accepted by*

HOUDINI

for the Second House, Friday night, May 2nd, at the

BIRMINGHAM EMPIRE

under the condition that the box is not air-tight.

When he had finished reading, Major Russell stabbed at the paper with an insistent forefinger. 'You initiated this?'

'It was my idea,' I replied. 'In those days I was working in my uncle's timber mill in Saltley for five shillings a week. I went to the "Empire" one night and was so impressed by Houdini's performance that I went backstage to see him after the show. He had announced that he would give a hundred pounds to anyone who could produce a wooden box from which he couldn't escape.'

'You accepted the challenge?'

'I certainly did. You see, Major, I assumed that the boxes he had used on the stage were not genuine. We had a first-class carpenter at the mill and I felt confident that he could knock something together that would baffle Houdini. To cut out any trickery, I stipulated that we should construct the box on the stage, in full view of the audience. Houdini agreed without any hesitation. The only snag was that he insisted on visiting the mill to meet our carpenter. As I dared not let my uncle know what I was up to, I had to fix the appointment during the lunch hour. I didn't realise at the time that by introducing Houdini to the carpenter, I was as good as throwing away any chance I had of winning that hundred pounds.'

'You mean he bribed him?'

I nodded ruefully. 'And I didn't find out until many years later at the Holborn "Empire", when Houdini was making his last appearance. He told me the whole story, but I'll come to that in a minute. All I remember seeing at the time was the arrival of a hansom cab, which drew up outside the office on a blazing hot summer's day, and out stepped Houdini, smoking a fat cigar and wearing a magnificent fur-lined coat and a pair of gaudy carpet slippers. He had a long chat with Ted Withers, our master carpenter, and then mystified me by pacing the full length of the sixty-foot wall at the front of the mill. I caught on next day, of course, and so did my uncle. Houdini's publicity agent had come back during the night and pasted an enormous bright yellow poster on the wall, calling attention to the challenge and generally advertising the Friday night show. Oh, he was a great showman was Harry Houdini!'

'And what happened at the performance?'

'First of all, Houdini told the audience that he had accepted the challenge of Messrs W. J. Clayton Limited. We next brought in the pieces of the box and Ted Withers assembled it on the stage to an orchestral accompaniment that was positively deafening. About twenty people came up, examined the finished job and pronounced it satisfactory. Some of them handcuffed Houdini, put him in a sack, sealed it, laid him inside the box, and Ted nailed down the lid. The whole thing was strongly roped, placed on a low trolley and wheeled into a small tent upstage. For the next ten to fifteen minutes the orchestra thumped out martial music *fortissimo*. Then, with dramatic suddenness, the curtains in front of the tent were swept aside, and Houdini, bathed in perspiration, stood there dangling the handcuffs from one hand and bowing to the wildly enthusiastic audience. The box was still intact and roped up as before.'

'It was the same box?' inquired Major Russell.

'Without any doubt. Not even the rope had been tampered with. The fellow who had actually tied the knot swore it had never been undone. It looked as though Houdini had achieved the impossible. Naturally, we didn't know that he had given Ted Withers three pounds to nail the box together in a certain way. In fact, there were only two full-length nails, top and bottom of the end from which he eventually emerged. Although the rest seemed all right, they penetrated only a single thickness of planking. All Houdini had to do, therefore, was to exert pressure with his feet and the end-piece pivoted on the two genuine nails. He cut himself free from the sack by means of a razor blade he had palmed when shaking hands with the last man to come up on the stage – a confederate. As an expert escapologist, he had no trouble in slipping out of the handcuffs. A moment or two later, he had fastened down the end, this time with proper nails, hammered in under cover of a Sousa march. Hammer and nails, by the way, were concealed in one of the bamboo poles that supported the tent. To all intents and purposes, nothing had been disturbed.'

'What about the slashed sack?' put in Major Russell astutely.

'Easily accounted for. To prove that there was nobody in the box, Houdini simply chopped it to pieces with an axe. When he finally produced the sack, the audience was not surprised by its torn condition. He thought of everything.'

'So you didn't get the hundred pounds, after all.'

'No, but Houdini *did* present me with what he referred to as "a fine silver watch" as a souvenir. It was only when I examined it later that I discovered that he had fooled me again. It was made of white metal and had no value whatsoever.'

At this point Major Russell abruptly thrust aside the mass of papers with which he had been dealing prior to my arrival, stood up and bade me follow him. 'You may be the very man we want,' he hinted mysteriously, as he conducted me along the murky corridor. 'Judging by what you've told me, I think you may very well fit into one of the square holes I mentioned. At any rate, we're looking

for a showman with an interest in escapology. You appear
to fill the bill.'

Wondering what it was all about, I accompanied my
guide out into the street and round to the old Metropole
Hotel, which had been taken over by the Office of Works.
There, in Room 424, a vast barn-like office on the fourth
floor, I was introduced to Major Crockatt – suave, well-
groomed, shrewd – who lost no time in informing me that
the only Scottish regiment worthy of the name was the
one to which he belonged – the Royal Scots – and that all
the best soldiers came from north of the border. At that
stage of our relationship I did not consider it expedient to
point out that most of the British Army's biggest battles
had been won by Irish generals. I merely eyed his many
decorations and murmured a polite agreement.

At the instigation of Major Russell, I repeated the gist
of my Houdini story and expressed a few forthright views
on the psychology of escape. As I finished, the two officers
exchanged significant glances.

'Good,' enthused Major Crockatt. 'I believe you'll do,
Hutton. But before we go any further, let me attempt to
put you in the picture. Our main concern in this department is to give assistance to prisoners-of-war. In the last
show, with a few notable exceptions, the men who were
captured by the enemy were content to stay put until the
cessation of hostilities. This present war is to be conducted
along vastly different lines. Not only will prisoners be
expected to seize all opportunities of escaping; the intention is also that they are to be supplied with gadgets that
will enable them to break out of the POW camps, and
once out, help them find their way to freedom.'

'But what about those that break out, and are captured
again?' I asked Major Crockatt.

'I was coming to that point,' he replied. 'It is one of

the reasons why it has been decided that all those who
are captured should try to escape, even if captured
again. The more that do this, the more upheaval they
can cause to their German captors. Of course wire-
cutters and saws, for instance, would be useful; so would
maps and compasses. The difficulty is that the obvious
escape aids are too big to be hidden. One of your headaches, then, will be concealment. Another will be the
invention of new escape material. Other problems will
undoubtedly crop up as the scheme develops. Now, do
you think you can cope?'

I replied unhesitatingly that I should be delighted to
try. Major Russell, who had been hovering in the background like a benevolent deity, then left us, and Major
Crockatt introduced me to the rest of his staff – a fascinating quartet of brilliant officers, who were to help me considerably at the outset of my curious assignment.

Our second-in-command, a major, was as tall as a
lamp-post and nearly as thin. Despite a quiet manner and
a voice so soft that it was frequently inaudible, he held
very decided views about the ultimate issue of the conflict, reiterating constantly that in the end the greatest
contributory factor to the defeat of the enemy would be
inadequate food stocks. The others had christened him
'Tiger,' but I never observed any resemblance between
the self-effacing major and that aggressive animal. When
I came to know him better, I concluded that the nickname originated from the way he would get his claws
firmly hooked into bureaucratic nonsense and hang on
until he had reduced it to a shambles.

In addition to this tenacity of purpose, he had a
thorough knowledge of the intricate workings of all three
services and a nice appreciation of the value of the 'old
boy' net-work. When trouble came later – usually as a

result of my unorthodox methods – the 'Tiger' always knew exactly which particular wire to pull on my behalf. Thanks to him, I was able to trespass frequently without fear of prosecution.

Another of our number, a small, wiry man with an impish sense of humour, had been secretary to one of the biggest investment trusts in the country. He now had charge of the funds allocated to the newly fledged escape organization. It was largely due to his ungrudging co-operation that I was destined to launch many costly schemes that at first shocked the controllers of high finance into niggardly opposition and automatic cheese-paring. He liked to laugh a lot, and when he was busy, he had a habit of singing quietly to himself.

The third member of the team acted as liaison officer between the Army and the Royal Air Force. Liaison between the Army and the Royal Navy was the responsi-bility of a large portly man with a typically nautical roll. He had a podgy genial face, generally with an engaging smile upon it, but he was to prove himself an exacting taskmaster. He, too, had been taken prisoner during the 1914–18 war, when the battleship on which he was serving had been sunk at Jutland. His prin-cipal pleasure, as time went on, was to twist my tail, if and whenever he could.

We were to be joined later in the year by two other men, one who had been for many years private secretary to Gordon Selfridge, who was put in charge of com-munications, and another whose chief occupation for many years had been sheep-farming in Chile. They both fitted admirably into the growing escape department, responding magnificently to my occasional appeals for advice or assistance.

After brief chats with my four colleagues I was taken

on one side by Major Crockatt and told to start work
straight away. 'I've decided to make you my technical
officer, Hutton. I'm afraid the best rank I can offer you
at present,' he said regretfully, 'is that of lieutenant.
Order your uniform as soon as possible, but don't
wear it unless it's absolutely essential. In this business a
certain amount of sartorial laxity has perforce to be
tolerated. I'm sure there's no need for me to enlarge on
the necessity for eternal vigilance and security-mindedness. And another thing – it will be better for all concerned if you carry out your work well away from this
office. Now, before you go, are there any points requiring
elucidation?'

'Just one question, sir. Have *you* any suggestions as to
how I set about my job?'

'It's entirely up to you,' was the disconcerting reply.
'There are no previous plans to work from and no official
records. You might do worse than read through the books
written by the escapers of the other war, but always bear
in mind that old ideas are no good at all. We want new
ones. So put on your thinking-cap, do as you like – and
I'll back you to the hilt.'

My head in a whirl and not a little awed by the magni-
tude of my task, I took my leave and made my way down
to the ground floor. As I emerged into the street, a hand
fell on my arm, almost startling me out of my wits. It
belonged to Johnny Evans. A scholar of great distinction,
with a remarkable knowledge of the Germans and their
characteristics, Evans was one of the few who had escaped
from enemy hands in the First World War. His hazardous
journey from Germany into Switzerland and his second
and more thrilling break-out from a Turkish fortress are
described with great gusto in his absorbing book, *The
Escaping Club*. It was Johnny Evans who, foreseeing

Germany's fresh bid for world domination, had taken the trouble to cycle to Switzerland between the wars for the purpose of photographing, from both sides of the border, the particular section of the German-Swiss frontier through which he had made his memorable march to freedom. His negatives of the Schaffhausen salient proved invaluable to us in our work later.

We chatted for at least an hour, and listening to my companion's sage counsel, I gradually regained my confidence. In fact, it was shortly after his departure that I began to discern dimly a method of tackling the vast problem that had been dropped into my lap.

'Remember this, Clutty,' had been Johnny Evans's final piece of advice, 'the best time for a man to escape is immediately after capture. There's precious little to be done for him once he's behind the wire. My own view is that every service man should be issued with three basic escape aids – a map, a compass, and food in a concentrated form – *before* he goes into battle. And if you can think of a way of concealing the map and the compass, so much the better.'

Maps, compasses and concentrated food packs, I agreed, would have to be given a high degree of priority. Before going into production, however, I had to have a blue print for escape. My obvious starting-point was the 1914–18 war. Despite the relatively few successful break-outs, the fact remained that the Germans had made certain provisions to prevent prisoners from escaping. By studying their technique then, I should be in a better position to estimate their probable lines of action in the new conflict. The more I learned about the enemy's previous security measures, the better I should be able to appreciate his present anti-escape precautions. In any event, if the German peace-time army in any way resembled the

British, it was quite on the cards that the military machine had undergone but little change.

It rather looked as though I had a heavy reading programme ahead of me. I grinned to myself at the prospect of spending the first few weeks of the second world war poring over dozens of critical works relating to the first. As I strolled briskly towards the West End, I resolved to pay a visit to the British Museum's extensive library on the following morning. In the meantime, I would go and see my tailor to be measured for a service dress.

Glancing at my wrist watch, I was surprised to find that only ninety minutes had elapsed since I had entered the War Office building. An hour and a half ago I had been a civilian. Now I was an Intelligence Officer and had been given a job that, on reflection, seemed quite divorced from reality. I had to provide escape gadgets for non-existent prisoners; I was expected to keep away from the concern that was employing me; I had to buy a uniform that I was not expected to wear. And my passport to the whole curious business had been a casual reference to my thwarted efforts to get the better of Harry Houdini, the world's greatest escapologist.

Lost in my musing, I almost bumped into a bespectacled schoolboy who was sauntering along with his eyes glued to the pages of an illustrated magazine. He simply accepted my apology and went on his way, but it was that brief encounter which sparked off an idea that was to save me long hours of irksome research and to furnish me with information without which Operation Escape Gadgets might never have been launched. There was no need for me to sift through the literature of the 1914–18 war. All I had to do was to get hold of all the relevant books, put them into the hands of a team of intelligent sixth-formers and ask them to note any passages appertaining to escape. I felt confident that the Chief Librarian at the British Museum would co-operate. The question was — which school should I approach with my unusual assignment?

I suddenly chuckled to myself. During my conversation with Johnny Evans, he had mentioned the public school attended by my Commanding Officer. Surely it was only fitting that Major Crockatt's *alma mater* should be invited to prepare the essential summaries.

Ten minutes later I was filling in a telegram form marked 'OHMS' in the Post Office near Trafalgar Square. It was addressed to the Headmaster of a well-known public school and its message was brief, mysterious and challenging: 'CALLING ON YOU TOMORROW AFTERNOON SIXTEEN HUNDRED HOURS TO DISCUSS PROJECT VITAL TO WAR EFFORT. — CLAYTON HUTTON.'

2   Silk Squares and Mulberry Leaves

Next morning, as I was about to leave the War Office for the British Museum, I was buttonholed in the corridor by a red-tabbed colonel who was a complete stranger to me.

'Are you Clayton Hutton?' he demanded peremptorily.

'I am, sir, but I don't think we've—'

'My name is Scott,' he cut in impatiently. 'I understand that you are interested in records relating to escapes and so on and that not a great deal of material is available.' The Colonel withdrew from his pocket a neatly folded document and thrust it into my hands. 'You may find this significant. It's a copy of a lecture delivered at Munich in 1937 by General von Brauchitsch. You'll find it has some bearing on the work you are to do.'

Waving aside my stammered thanks, the Colonel stumped off down the corridor. I put the typescript in my pocket and proceeded to the British Museum. Within a few minutes of my arrival I was closeted with the Chief Librarian, explaining to him exactly what I was after. Friendly, courteous and co-operative, he immediately arranged for most of the World War One escape books to be collected from the shelves and placed at my disposal. From these I selected the ones which I considered relevant to my scheme and intimated that I should like to borrow them. The Chief Librarian regretted that he could not allow me to take the books away with me, but he was delighted to detail two assistants to scour the second-hand bookshops and publishing houses to purchase copies on my behalf.

Whilst the assistant librarians were chasing escape books, I made my way to a nearby café. Over a cup of

coffee I read through the document given to me by
Colonel Scott. It was a report on the spying and sabotage
activities of enemy prisoners, more particularly the
French, during the first war. It made fascinating reading.

The first part of the report revealed that General
Dupont had promulgated a decree instructing prisoners-of-
war to defy the Germans at all times. Collaborators would
be punished and saboteurs richly rewarded once Germany
was beaten. According to von Brauchitsch, the French
prisoners had responded enthusiastically to their General's
spirited words. Compelled to work in factories, they had
thrown sand into the machinery; forced to labour in the
fields, they had contrived to ruin the potato crop. If von
Brauchitsch was to be believed, the volatile Frenchmen
had even tried to sabotage German morale. I was
especially impressed, however, by the many references to
sabotage equipment and to messages being smuggled into
the POW camps, and by the organization of escapes that
was part of the same policy.

Then came what was, as far as I was concerned, the
very crux of von Brauchitsch's lecture. 'The most vital
preparations consisted in obtaining possession of mapping
materials, compasses, forged permits, wire cutters and a
supply of food. By means of printed guides and maps
smuggled in (concealed in gift parcels) the routes chosen
for an escape were reproduced.' The compasses, he added,
were either concealed in foodstuffs sent from abroad or
made by the men themselves from pieces of magnetized
metal. Relatives of British prisoners, it appeared, often
smuggled in escaping equipment inside tins of food.

When I reached the end of this excellent document, it
was time to return to the Chief Librarian's office. The two
assistants were already back and copies of fifty escape
books were lying there, done up in bundles of ten.

After the volumes of escape material had been transferred to the back seat of my car, I thanked the Chief
Librarian and his assistants and took my leave. I headed
for Marble Arch and was soon speeding along the A-5 on
an eighty-odd-mile journey to the Midlands. Dozens of
ideas were flitting through my mind, but my main concern was the sort of reception I should get at the public
school.

I need not have worried. The Headmaster listened most
sympathetically to my proposals, appreciated the importance of the extra-curricular tasks his pupils would be
called upon to perform, despatched a party of boys to
remove the books from my car, and promised that my
requirements would be met within four days. I drove
back to London full of confidence and not a little proud
of my achievements.

Whilst waiting for the escape blueprint to be drawn up,
I found plenty to do. I established myself in a small room
in the War Office building itself, acquired what I could
in the way of furniture and equipment, and made such
personal contacts as would stand me in good stead later
on. In accordance with Major Crockatt's instructions, I
kept strictly away from the Hotel Metropole, except on
the rare occasions when my requests to other sections
needed the approval of 'higher authority'.

When I reported to the Headmaster of the public school
on the fourth day after my first visit, I was presented with
a sheaf of typescripts, each containing an admirable *précis*
of the contents of one or other of the fifty volumes I had
left there. In no case did an abridgement run to more than
two pages and the youthful research team had even gone
to the trouble of preparing four copies for me. A glance at
the top sheet told me that the boys had taken the job
seriously. Everything was set out neatly and concisely

under chapter headings and the salient points were in block capitals. My roving eye fell on a list of desirable escape aids – dyes, wire, needles, copying paper, saws, and a dozen other items, some of which I should never have dreamed of – and I knew right away that as technical officer to the Escape Department I was in for a very busy time indeed.

I thanked the Headmaster for his assistance and asked him to convey my gratitude to those pupils who had laboured on my behalf. The books were carried to my car, and with the precious typescripts on the seat beside me, I was soon weaving in and out of the busy A-5 traffic. Three hours later, I was comfortably ensconced in an arm-chair in my flat, with a writing-pad balanced on my knee, summarizing the summaries. By three o'clock in the morning my master plan was ready.

Next day I charged unceremoniously into Major Crockatt's office and asked my chief where I could get a map of Germany. He advised me curtly to try the Map Room. Warned by the note of asperity in his voice, I beat an immediate retreat and hurried round to the War Office. One of the aged commissionaires gave me the location of the map department, and never imagining for a moment that I was about to meet with my first set-back, I threaded the maze of corridors with one object in view – to obtain a map of Germany, scaled to one over two million.

There was a notice on the door of the Map Room – 'MOST SECRET. KEEP OUT.' I knocked for form's sake and walked in. Before I had advanced three paces into the room, I was seized by an enormous red-headed major and hustled smartly back into the corridor.

'Can't you read?' barked my assailant, pointing to the unequivocal warning.

I mumbled insincere apologies and was about to slink

sheepishly away. Then it suddenly struck me that I had
seen the major before somewhere. Frantically I searched
my memory and eventually I got it. He was the son of
Lieutenant-General Sir Francis Festing, one of our best-
known generals of the 1914–18 war: it had been his
father, as a matter of fact, who had taught me how to fly.
He gave a start of astonishment when I addressed him by
name and mentioned that I had last seen him on top of a
bus, being taken by his father to attend a cadet course at
Aldershot. He must have been only sixteen at the time.

It was a lucky coincidence for me. As soon as I told him
who I was, the major's whole attitude softened and without more ado he invited me into the holy of holies. He
was now affability personified. Unfortunately he could
not supply me with the map I was seeking. 'We haven't
a single map of Germany to the scale you require,' he
announced with regret. 'I doubt if you'll get one in the
Army at all. You might try the RAF and the Navy, but
I'm afraid I can't hold out much hope of success.'

I wandered off disconsolately to try the other two arms
of the service. For some days I pestered the heads of
dozens of departments, but the result was invariably the
same. I came away empty-handed.

In desperation I decided to call on Geographia Limited
in Fleet Street and tell them what I was looking for. Once
again I drew a blank, for they had no suitable map in
print. They did suggest, however, that I should try
a famous Scottish firm.

I have never believed that really important matters can
be settled by letter-writing, so by telephoning here and
there to a few influential friends at the Air Ministry, I
arranged to fly to Scotland on the following morning.

When I reached Edinburgh, a taxi took me to the firm,
where I demanded to see somebody who was empowered

to make a certain decision in connection with the copyright of certain continental maps. Without hesitation I
was introduced to the managing director – a friendly,
forthright Scotsman, with an appreciation of priorities and
a fine determined chin. A quiet reference to security
obviously had its effect, but I told him nothing of the
escape organization. I simply asked for maps of Germany,
France, Poland, Italy, Austria, Switzerland, Belgium,
Holland and all Balkan countries and stated bluntly that
my intention was to reproduce them by the thousand.
Not only did he hand me all the maps I wanted; he also
begged me to forget the whole question of copyright.
It was a privilege, he insisted, to contribute to the war
effort.

'Tell me,' I said to him, 'what would have happened if
I had bought the maps in the normal way and had copies
made without consulting you? How could you possibly
know that your copyright had been infringed? After all,
other firms are in this business and one map of, say,
Germany, must be exactly like another.'

The managing director chuckled and shook his head.
'That's just where you're wrong, Mr Hutton. There is
something quite distinctive about our maps. Those of us
who are in the know can identify one on sight.'

'How?' I persisted.

'Well, it's something of a trade secret, but I imagine all
map-makers play the same sort of trick on their customers, so there's no real harm in putting you in the
picture. Every single map we produce here contains a
deliberate mistake – small, unimportant, but easily detected if one knows where to look for it. So you see, Mr
Hutton, if you'd copied one of our maps, you wouldn't
have got away with it.'

After pointing out and explaining the minor geographical discrepancies on several of the firm's maps, the managing director talked at great length on the special techniques of the skilled cartographer. Once embarked on his favourite subject, he could not resist tracing the historical background of map-making from the early efforts of the ancient Egyptians and Greeks right up to the perfectly scaled representations turned out in the twentieth century. I learned how Eratosthenes first measured the length of a degree and how Ptolemy made his revolutionary net-work of parallels and meridians. I listened spellbound to an account of the methods used to minimise the distortion that was inevitable because the earth's surface is curved, whilst maps are flat. At school I had been taught something about Mercator's Projection; at the end of the managing director's fascinating lecture, I really understood what it all meant.

During the return journey I gloated over the maps and pondered over my next move. I knew there would be no difficulty over reproduction. A friend of mine, Bernard Attenborough, who worked for C. & E. Layton Limited, a firm of blockmakers and printers in London, could easily arrange for thousands of copies to be produced. The problem was where to obtain the kind of paper that was necessary. It had to be so thin that it would take up next to no room when folded, and at the same time it had to be fairly durable and crease-resisting. Most important of all, if the maps were to be hidden in service uniforms, they would not have to rustle.

For several days I experimented and made exhaustive inquiries at paper manufacturers all over London, but all my efforts came to nought. C. & E. Layton Limited, for instance, furnished me with a number of beautifully turned-out maps on paper no thicker than that of the finest toilet roll, but unfortunately the finished articles

proved impracticable for one of two reasons. Either they
rustled abominably, or after being folded up small for a
few hours, they were rendered illegible along the creases.
As it became increasingly clear that suitable paper was
apparently unobtainable, I began to think in terms of
another medium – silk.

My only connection with the silk industry was a nodding acquaintance with one of the big Macclesfield manufacturers – a man called Wallace Ellison. I promptly rang
him up and asked for an immediate appointment to discuss a highly confidential matter linked up with silk
supplies for the services. When he pressed me for further
information, I sternly reminded him that telephone lines
could be tapped. What I had to say was for his ears alone.
Somehow I managed to imply that his co-operation could
make all the difference between victory and defeat.

My luck was in. Mr Ellison told me that he had an
engagement in London on the following day. He suggested
that we should dine together at the Bath Club. Finally it
was decided that we should meet in the bar at seven
o'clock for a pre-prandial *apéritif*.

Sipping our Dubonnets next day, Ellison and I fenced
warily until we had established our *bona fides* each to
the other's satisfaction. Then we went in to dinner, con-
tinuing with our still mildly evasive tactics until we had
reached the coffee and brandy stage of what had been a
magnificent meal. Up to that moment I had not even
hinted at our special interest in prisoners-of-war and the
steps we were taking to provide them with escape
material. I was all the more surprised, therefore, when
my host, who had been reminiscing about his experiences
in the first world war, casually mentioned that he was
the author of a book called *Escapes and Adventures*, dealing with escapers from German camps during the 1914–

18 period. I was so taken aback by this reference to a subject which I had been carefully avoiding that I was convinced there had been a leakage of information. As the conversation developed, however, I realized that Ellison was completely in the dark as far as our escape plans were concerned.

On learning that he had been a prisoner himself, I decided to come clean – or at least fairly clean. I began by reading the Official Secrets Act to him and then went on to explain why I had sought him out. Without giving away anything of vital importance, I described our escape plans in general terms, told him of my difficulties in regard to maps, and asked for his expert views on the possibility of printing maps on silk.

The man from Macclesfield confessed that he personally had never heard of such a process, but he saw no reason why it should not be carried out. He put forward two or three tentative ideas and then whisked me off to his London office, handed me three dozen white silk squares and advised me to experiment on them. He promised that if ever I should hit on a successful method, he would ensure that the requisite amount of silk would be made available for me. His firm's stocks were all bespoken, but if the necessity arose, he could furnish me with certain addresses. By the time I left him, he was as enthusiastic about the project as I was myself.

Working all the next day, it was nearly midnight when my printer friend and I gloomily surveyed the silk squares we had ruined. All our attempts to print maps in eight colours had failed. Each time the silk was lifted from the 'bed of the printing machine, we found that the ink had run, blurring outlines and rendering place names illegible. It was beginning to look as though the silk map was not a practical proposition.

For days we tried to find a satisfactory solution to our problem, but nothing could induce the coloured inks to 'sit' on the silk. Then, as a last resort, I wondered if a little pectin – a gummy substance found in certain fruits and roots to which the setting power of jams is due – would serve as an agent to coagulate the ink and prevent it from running. Without any real faith in what we were doing, my friend and I prepared the new mixture and put it to the test. Our spirits soared when we gazed down at the resultant print. It was perfect down to the last detail. Even the smallest topographical feature was sharply defined. The escaper's most important accessory would soon be ready for issue.

A later development was to treat the silk map with powdered chalk, lay it on a cardboard base and feed it into the machine a second time, thus achieving a double printing – France on one side and Germany on the other. A telephone call to Wallace Ellison provided me with the location of a parachute factory just outside London and there I obtained several bales of silk for my 21-inch squares. The transaction was indicative of the change that had come over the country's commercial standards since the outbreak of war. When I offered to pay lavishly for the silk, nobody was interested. As soon as I mentioned that I had a number of cases of jam and marmalade, unused samples from my pre-war stock, stored in my garage, the deal was completed without further quibbling.

Although maps identical to mine were on sale quite openly in a shop I knew in Fleet Street and doubtless elsewhere, I was prompted by some imp of mischief to stamp my silk copies 'MOST SECRET'. This gratuitous addition led to an amusing incident that might have ended disastrously for the individual concerned. It occurred shortly after I had started to issue my maps to the RAF.

I was sitting in my office one day when the telephone rang, and on picking up the receiver, I heard a coldly precise voice say, 'To whom am I speaking, please?' When I told the caller who I was, he went on, 'I should like to see you. You don't know me, but it is essential I meet you at once.'

Assuming that one of my friends was attempting to take a rise out of me, I replied flippantly, suggesting a rendezvous at midnight at the top of Nelson's column in Trafalgar Square. My mysterious caller persisted, however, in tones of such urgency that I finally consented to an appointment in a well-known building not very far from Whitehall. I strolled round to the meeting-place and was ushered into a dingy, ill-lit basement room, in which the only furniture consisted of a desk, a chair, and over in one corner, a wooden box. I was eyeing my drab surroundings with distaste when the door opened to admit two men of forbidding appearance. There was something about their bearing and the cut of their suit that led me to believe they were plain-clothes detectives.

After my identity had been established, the older man of the two offered me a cigarette and moved ponderously to his desk chair. His confederate sauntered casually towards the upturned box and sat down. I was left standing uncomfortably in the middle of the room.

The senior man introduced himself – he *was* a detective – and then went on, 'We are investigating a matter that may very well turn out to be extremely serious. We understand you will be able to help us in our inquiries.'

Irritated by the deliberately contrived atmosphere of pseudo-secrecy, I said, 'Now, look here, if I can help you, I will, but I refuse to subscribe to this *deuxième bureau* farce. For a start you can get rid of your jack-on-the-box there or you won't get a word out of me.'

The younger man glared at me venomously, but at a nod from his superior he rose to his feet and stamped out. When he had gone, I startled my interrogator by demanding his solemn assurance that there were no microphones concealed in the room. Satisfied on this point, I strolled over to the corner, sat down on the box and lit the cigarette he had given me. Flicking the match stick on to the dusty floor, I waited for the detective to begin.

He said nothing, however, but he lifted his blotter, and with a theatrical gesture, whipped from beneath it one of my silk maps of Germany. For a moment I felt quite nonplussed.

'Where do you think I picked this up?' he asked at last.

I shook my head dumbly.

'This map came into my possession in a pub near Harrow – last night,' he said impressively. 'I saw a young flying officer take it from his pocket and hand it over to his girl friend. When they were leaving, she employed it as a head scarf. As they passed me on their way out, I spotted that it was a map of Germany and that it was marked "MOST SECRET". I'm afraid some of these young fliers aren't as security-conscious as they ought to be. Anyway, I confiscated the map and reported the matter. The youngster's Commanding Officer referred me to you.'

'Good God!' I exclaimed. 'I hope you're not going to prefer charges.'

The detective looked down at the map and shrugged. 'After all, sir, such carelessness could lead to a serious leakage. It wouldn't be so bad if the thing wasn't on the Secret List.'

To his astonishment I roared with laughter. 'Come with me and I'll show you something that may change your views. I take it you have a car outside?'

A few minutes later we pulled up outside a stationer's shop in Fleet Street. I led my companion to the window and pointed to one of Bartholomew's cycling maps of Germany. Then I told him that the original of the "Most Secret" silk map he had just shown me was on sale to the general public. To my relief he saw the humour of the situation, promised to do what he could for the young officer and we parted on amicable terms.

I heard afterwards that the youthful offender had got off with a lecture on security-mindedness. Two years later he won the DFC.

I had not entirely abandoned my idea of printing the escape maps on paper, for quite apart from my desire to run the gadget business as economically as possible, I could foresee that a time might come when silk would be wholly diverted to the parachute industry. We experimented with all available types of paper and actually discovered one that did not rustle when screwed up. It was not the perfect answer, but we made use of it because at the time we could produce nothing better.

Then I met a man I shall call Bravada and my search for the right paper was at an end.

It was my habit to lunch at my club in Piccadilly. I went there for two very sound reasons: the food was better and cheaper; the other members were or had been airmen. As an ex-flier, I found the company of fighter and bomber pilots peculiarly stimulating. We talked the same language and shared a common interest in the rapidly expanding Royal Air Force.

For some days I had been aware of a young fellow in his early thirties, who also lunched at the club and who invariably gave me a friendly nod or wave, although I could not for the life of me place him. He always wore civilian clothes, so I had no clue as to his rank or official position. His lunchtime acknowledgments teased me beyond endurance, for I had a guilty feeling that I had seen his face somewhere before. Identification eluded me, however, until one day, when I was enjoying the sunshine in Green Park, he fell into step alongside me, and addressing me familiarly by my nickname, went on to ask me how my gadgetry was progressing.

I was thrown immediately on my guard, for my work so far had been a behind-the-scenes activity. 'What do *you* know about it?' I demanded sharply.

To my amazement he knew quite a lot about my schemes, for he had seen and admired my silk maps and he slyly congratulated me on the ease with which I had short-circuited the official supply system. His name, he concluded, was Bravada.

Convinced by his knowledgeable manner that he was thoroughly reliable, I chatted freely about my contribution thus far to the escape problem. I described my early difficulties and how I had gradually overcome them. But it was when I was sketching my plans for the future that I detected a quickening of Bravada's interest. He gripped my arm excitedly as soon as I mentioned the paper I needed.

'I think I can be of assistance,' he informed me. 'Paper is not normally my pigeon, but according to my intelligence staff, I may very well be involved in a paper-chase within the next few days. If you can spare half an hour, I'll show you exactly what I mean.'

My curiosity aroused, I accompanied him to a new block of offices less than a mile from Piccadilly. Mr Bravada conducted me to his own particular department. We passed through an outer room in which were seated several smartly dressed young ladies, alert and for the most part attractive. On each girl's desk was a confusing array of telephones of different colours. When I entered the luxuriously appointed inner room, which was clearly Mr Bravada's private office, I was at once struck by the huge painting of a reclining nude that occupied almost the whole of one wall. My guide, unseen by me, must have pressed some hidden button or switch, for this painting slowly swung open to reveal a solid wooden door. He opened it and we stepped through into an enormous room beyond.

On the metalled walls were painted the seas and oceans of the world, and dotted about on the wide expanses of deep blue, were hundreds of tiny, magnetically treated ships. Working in this magnificent chamber were another half-dozen lovelies, as *chic* and as streamlined as those in the first office. Their not very onerous duties lay in moving the miniature vessels about with the aid of long pointers whenever messages were brought in by the team of telephonists outside.

Bravada was evidently enjoying my undisguised bewilderment. 'As the White Knight said, "It's my own invention",' he remarked with a grin. 'Come into my parlour and I'll tell you all about it.'

Comfortably ensconced in an armchair, with my back to the disturbing nude, I listened, entranced, to Bravada's fantastic story. Occasionally a trim shape flitted silently through the room, doubtless with information of some unexpected deviation in a vessel's course, and I knew that on one of the wall charts a magnetized model would be steered into her new position. At first I was distracted by the interruptions, but soon my host's narrative so enthralled me that I was no longer conscious of the comings and goings. The distant hum of London's traffic faded and the only sound was the hypnotic murmur of Bravada's voice.

He told me that for many years the members of his family had been connected with the diamond industry and consequently they knew all the important diamond merchants on the Continent. On the outbreak of war, Bravada had reasoned that the top-ranking Nazis would attempt, as a precautionary measure, to cache large currency reserves in various neutral countries. Now, long experience had taught him that one of the most practicable methods of transferring large assets clandestinely from one country to another was that of diamond smuggling. The Nazis, he felt sure, would convert part of their wealth into diamonds and attempt to run the British blockade.

After getting official backing, he had built up a vast network of which his London office was the nerve centre. His Continental agents sent in reports of all big diamond deals carried out by the Germans in cities such as Brussels or Amsterdam, and thereafter every move of the purchaser was carefully checked. So efficient was Bravada's European organization that whenever a parcel of diamonds left Germany *en route* for, say, Lisbon or Barcelona or South America, certain information would flow in through one of the coloured telephones, and a few seconds later, a little metal ship would start its day-by-day voyage across the ocean wall.

Meanwhile the real ship would be scudding over the face of the waters with the diamond smuggler among its passengers. The trip would be uneventful until, without warning, a British submarine would surface within hailing distance and signal to the captain that a boarding party would like to visit his vessel. The foreign captain, recognizing the futility of resistance, would wisely accede to this request. The British senior officer of the boarding party would then ask to see Herr——, the diamond smuggler, interrogate him and examine his papers (which would be as false as the name under which he would be travelling). Apparently satisfied, he would bid the captain a pleasant good-day and return with his men to the waiting submarine, leaving behind a very relieved but greatly puzzled Herr———.

But the smuggler's troubles would only just be beginning, for on the following day a British gunboat would appear over the horizon and issue unequivocal orders to the foreign ship to stop. Mystified by this second visit, the captain would welcome the British officers aboard and discover to his surprise that they, too, were interested in Herr———. By that time he would be cursing the day he accepted the German as a passenger.

Again the smuggler would be questioned, but with a difference. He would be told bluntly that his statements were not believed, that his papers were irregular and that he was carrying contraband in the shape of diamonds. Realizing that the game was up, he would either hand over his precious cargo or seek the protection of the ship's captain. The captain, under threat of being escorted to an allied port, would naturally recommend co-operation. In any case, the interception would prove successful and diamonds intended to feather a foreign nest for some Nazi big-shot would thus be diverted to help finance the British war effort.

When Bravada had concluded his amazing account of what virtually amounted to piracy on the high seas, I began to ask myself how my quest for non-rustling paper supplies fitted into such a scheme. I was so awed by the immense powers he could set in motion that I hesitated to remind him of his earlier reference to a paper-chase. It was Bravada himself who reverted to the matter.

'I can see you are wondering how I can help you,' he

said. 'Well, it so happens that for some days we have
been plotting the course of a small Japanese ship, which
is carrying amongst her cargo something that interests us.
She is also carrying a peculiar type of pulp made from
mulberry leaves and I have it on very good authority that
from this pulp can be made an extremely thin but incredibly strong kind of paper. Now, according to all the
evidence, that ship is heading for waters where we can
easily arrange interception. I fancy that the captain could
be – er – induced to make for one of our ports. I think he
could also be persuaded to present us with – amongst
other things – his cargo of pulp. Does the prospect please
you?'

'Please me!' I exclaimed. 'It intoxicates me!'

'Good. Then leave the affair in my hands and I'll do my
best for you. If all goes well, you should be hearing from
me within the next two or three days. Should I miss you
at the club, I'll give you a ring.'

Waving aside my pæan of gratitude, Bravada escorted
me to the street. Already visualizing the many uses to
which the Japanese paper could be put, I proceeded
happily homewards, whilst my self-appointed ally returned to his midget fleets and their delightful navigators.

Bravada was not at the club for the next two days, but
on the morning of the third day the phone rang in my
office. The Mikado's compliments, a cool impersonal voice
announced, and bags of a certain commodity were awaiting to be collected at Dover. Could I arrange the necessary
transport? It would be advisable to provide the driver of
the leading vehicle with documentary proof that he had
been sent by me. Did I wish to ask any questions?

I had only one query. What was the approximate
weight of the load?

The tonnage quoted staggered me. I went hurrying off

to the appropriate department and in less than an hour a convoy of three-tonners might have been seen crossing Vauxhall Bridge, rolling out of London. Even before the trucks were on the move, I was in conference with a group of scientists at a nearby paper-mill. I explained the probable nature of the pulp consignment I was expecting and specified what qualities I was seeking in the paper that was soon to be manufactured. It was a long and highly technical discussion that lasted well into the afternoon. If the Japanese pulp belonged to one of several categories, the odds were strongly in favour of my requirements being met. The outlook was decidedly promising.

When the lorries returned, little time was lost in producing the first samples of the new paper. I jigged about like an excited schoolboy as I watched test after test. The results were sensational. Although it was so transparent that one could see the moon through it, the Japanese paper proved unbelievably strong. Maps in seven colours could be printed legibly on both sides. It was possible to soak the paper in water, screw it into a ball and then smooth it out so that the surface showed hardly a crease. Most important of all, when I picked up a sheet and crumpled it in my fist, it did not rustle.

My brief-case bulging with my latest paper maps, I called on an old friend of mine who owned a printing firm that specialized in the manufacture of Christmas cards. Twenty-odd years had passed since I had given him his first lesson in flying, but he had not forgotten his earlier indebtedness to me. There was genuine warmth in his welcome and his face lit up when I told him I urgently needed his help. Expressing his readiness to be of service, he waited impatiently while I unbuckled my case and fished out a bundle of maps. I laid one of the thin paper squares on his desk and pointed to it.

'This job is really going to tax your ingenuity,' I warned him. 'I want that map fitted between two ordinary sheets of paper in such a way that it will remain secure and undetected under a normal investigation and yet, when it is required, it must be easily accessible. Is that a practical possibility?'

For answer he pressed a bell and a few seconds later one of his employees appeared. The young fellow listened intelligently whilst my friend told him what had to be done, shook his head dubiously, and after examining the flimsy paper map, announced that he would look into the matter. Perhaps the gentleman would let him have a few maps to experiment on and then call back in a week's time.

When I returned to the workshop the following week and asked my friend if he had anything to report, he smiled mysteriously and indicated several rolls of brown paper lying on a table. I smoothed out one of the rolls and carefully scrutinized the edges. If a map was concealed therein, I could find no indication of its presence. I even tore the sheet into four strips and inspected each piece. Superficially, at any rate, they presented nothing out of the ordinary. I began to suspect that my leg was being pulled.

Meanwhile my friend had rung for the young man with whom I had left my maps. He came in carrying a bucket of water. Taking one of the brown paper strips, he dropped it into the bucket and thoroughly immersed it. For a while nothing happened. Then, with startling suddenness, the paper curled up into two coils and from between the two layers a portion of my map floated to the surface of the water.

'The magicians don't know it all,' remarked the young technician quietly.

Congratulating him on his skill and perseverance, I fished out the fragment of map, dried it quickly between two sheets of blotting-paper and pored over the two surfaces. All the names and topographical features were clearly distinguishable. Whatever new-fangled adhesive had been used, it had not affected legibility.

I left behind hundreds of maps to be similarly treated; those which had already been doctored I bore back in triumph to my office. I had silk maps, paper maps that did not rustle, and now cunningly concealed maps for special purposes. My mind was already busy with plans for the provision of the map reader's indispensable companion.

The compass. . . .

3 'Swinging' in the Old Kent Road

Although temperamentally opposed to orthodox methods, I thought it was perhaps advisable to start my compass campaign by consulting the gunnery experts at the War Office. I was by no means surprised when they showed me instruments about the size of my grandfather's gold watch. Not for a moment had I imagined that they would have produced the miniature compass I had in mind. I was not even perturbed by their reiterated assurances that their Brobdingnagian contraptions were the smallest available. I merely smiled politely and went away to try sources of supply other than 'proper channels'.

I first visited Negretti and Zambra, London's most famous firm of instrument makers. Mr Negretti listened sympathetically to what I had to say, but regretted that he was too busy with Government contracts to attend to my requirements. He ventured the opinion that a compass need not necessarily be an outsize affair and advised me to go to a factory he knew of in North London.

Half an hour later I was sitting in the manager's office at the North London factory. Before I left I was promised delivery of fifty specially made compasses, not more than half an inch in diameter. In due course they arrived at my flat, but they were no good. The needles fell off.

Picking up the London classified telephone directory, I thumbed through its pages until I found a list of scientific instrument makers. My first intention was to call on each firm in alphabetical order and stick at it until I struck one willing to co-operate, but I changed my plans when I noticed that only one was printed in bold black type. I resolved to do business with them.

Crossing the Thames by Blackfriars Bridge, I drove to what appeared to be a row of shabby old houses in the Old Kent Road, and with a certain amount of misgiving, entered a poky little office. I brightened up considerably on meeting the two remarkable old gentlemen who owned the factory. Although they must have been getting on for seventy years of age, the Blunt brothers looked incredibly fit and mentally alert. They quickly grasped what I was after, expressed their belief that my demands could be met, and handed me over to one of their right-hand men, George Waterlow, with whom I was soon on the friendliest of terms.

I rubbed my eyes in amazement when I was shown what lay behind that unprepossessing façade. I was ushered into a beautifully equipped scientific instrument laboratory, where I was introduced to a staff of highly skilled craftsmen. In the spacious workshops at least two thousand men were employed. I was also presented to another delightful personality – Dick Richards – who proved as amiable and as eager to assist as his colleague.

George and Dick promised to make me five thousand compasses within a week, if I provided a sufficient quantity of steel strip which could be magnetized. It would certainly mean, they agreed, a trip to Sheffield.

'How much would you like?' I asked casually.

George and Dick exchanged amused glances. They were clearly of the opinion that I was trying to be funny. 'Well, we'd *like* a thousand feet,' said George, as he winked at Dick, 'but it'll be a miracle if you get hold of a hundred. There's a war on, you know.'

'It's because there's a war on that I propose to let you have a thousand feet,' I asserted. I glanced at my watch and then added, 'In fact, it will be here tomorrow morning at ten o'clock!'

The two experts were still laughing at my rash pre-
diction when I took my leave. Perhaps they would not
have been quite so amused if they could have seen me
speed to Croydon airport. Luck was with me, for in less
than an hour I was airborne and on my way to Sheffield.
On reaching my destination, I rushed round to the biggest
steel works in the city, haggled for form's sake with the
manager, temptingly referred to my jam and marmalade
stocks, reluctantly agreed to the price he demanded, and
within an hour of my plane touching down, I had bought
a thousand feet of steel strip.

Cut up into convenient lengths, the steel strips were
loaded there and then and the lorry that was to transport
them to London left Sheffield that same day. The driver
was instructed to travel through the night and to report
to me at the War Office not later than nine o'clock on
the following morning. I completed the whole transaction
in good time to catch a return flight to Croydon.

Next day I convoyed the lorry from the War Office to
the Old Kent Road factory and effected delivery, as
scheduled, at ten o'clock. George Waterlow's face was a
study as he watched the steel being offloaded. I thoroughly
enjoyed my little triumph. 'Let me know when you've
worked through that,' I mocked him, 'and I'll order
another thousand feet.'

But seven days after receiving the steel, George and
Dick showed me that I was not the only one who could
keep a promise. I had dropped in on them to inquire how
Operation Compass was progressing, but before I could
frame my opening question, George invited me to hold
out my hand. Wonderingly I did so. With the enigmatic
air of a conjuror, George dropped a tiny metal object into
my palm. It was a narrow steel bar, almost an inch in
length, with two luminous dots at one end and only one

at the other. A neat hole had been drilled in the middle.

'Your first compass,' said George quietly. 'You hang it on a thread, wait for it to stop swinging, and you'll find the arm with the two dots is pointing due north. Any good?'

Any good? It was superb and exactly what I had hoped for – small, accurate and cheap to manufacture. I asked George how many had been made.

'Five thousand,' he replied, and then continued with a sly grin, 'and if you let me know when you need any more, we'll knock off another five thousand. But come into the factory and inspect the latest gadget.'

George ushered me into one of the work-rooms and steered me towards a table at the far end. Scattered about the table were tools of every description, scraps of metal, gauges, and a number of drawings and tracings. Amongst all this crazy miscellany was a wooden tray and in the centre of the tray lay a short brass cylinder not more than a quarter of an inch in diameter. George picked it up between thumb and forefinger and held it out towards me.

I gasped with admiration. The cylinder was hollow, and inside it, delicately quivering, a fine needle was balanced underneath a transparent protective cover. I glanced inter-rogatively at George.

'Yes, it's a compass,' he vouchsafed, 'and it's dead accu-rate. We're still working on it, but when it's finished, it'll be the smallest we've ever made. Is it going to be of any use to you?'

'Any use?' I echoed. 'Why, a compass that size will be invaluable. Just think of the thousand and one places in which it can be hidden. I'm sure it will fit into a cigarette, for instance.'

'It certainly will,' agreed George, 'because we've tried it! *And* inside the stem of a pipe.'

It was at that moment, as I was staring down fascinatedly at the 'baby' compass, that a wonderful idea flashed across my mind. 'I've got it, George!' I exclaimed involuntarily. 'We'll manufacture compasses that screw into the backs of service buttons. Every soldier and every airman in future will carry his own passport to freedom on his uniform, in the shape of a compass button. The question is – can you do it?'

'You produce the buttons and we'll fit them with compasses. We want something slightly larger than this, and possibly not quite so deep.' George tapped the compass he was still holding and added tentatively, 'I should imagine this type of thing might very easily be modified to go inside one of those little forage cap buttons.'

From then onwards there was no restraining the enthusiasm of my good friends at Messrs Blunt's. Although the factory had been concentrating on the production of bombsights ever since the beginning of the war, time was somehow found to supply me with everything I asked for in the compass line, and for many other gadgets besides, for as long as the escape department continued to operate. Ordinary bar compasses, tunic button compasses, fly button compasses, collar stud compasses, 'threepenny-bit' compasses, every conceivable kind of miniature compass, first in thousands and later in millions, came in a steadily increasing stream from the Old Kent Road factory as the war progressed.

George Waterlow, Dick Richards and I soon came to view anything metallic in terms of 'swing'. We magnetized everything that could possibly help a prisoner-of-war – pen and pencil clips, pen nibs, fountain pen filler levers, darning needles. But the most ingenious idea of all was put forward by Dick Richards one afternoon as we were strolling together through the factory.

'Look here, Clutty,' he began. 'You're always asking for compasses. Now, this morning I hit on a scheme whereby you can have them by the million and it won't cost you a penny.'

It seemed too good to be true, but I asked Dick to explain.

'It's simple, man,' he said impatiently. 'I don't know why one of us didn't think of it before. Every man in the forces uses a safety razor, doesn't he? I'm sure that safety razor blades can be sent to prisoners, in their parcels, without being checked. So all you have to do is to persuade the razor blade manufacturers to magnetize the steel from which their products are made. Then every blade becomes a compass. Like this!'

And so saying, Dick carefully fished a folded sheet of paper from his pocket. Opening up the paper, he revealed a Gillette safety razor blade attached by the centre hole to a length of thread. He suspended the blade in the air. We watched it spin round for a moment or two, until at last it settled down and remained steady.

'You see,' said Dick. 'It's pointing due north.'

'Yes, but by the same token the other end is pointing due south,' I objected. 'How are you going to tell which is which without putting a mark on the blade?'

'No trouble at all. All you have to do is to let the capital letter in the maker's name – "G", for example, in Gillette, or "M" in Myatt – represent the northern pointer. No special mark is necessary.'

It was undoubtedly a brilliant conception. Two of the most famous razor blade manufacturers in the country accepted our proposals without demur and magnetized their blades as a matter of course right through until the end of the war. Service personnel were informed during unit lectures and it did not take long for the notion that

every blade was a compass to penetrate to most formations of the Army and Air Force.

Needless to say, we continued to produce our compasses
in the factory. For one thing, they were more reliable
than the magnetized razor blades; for another, they were
easier to conceal; then again, they were altogether handier
and less likely to attract attention than dangling oblongs
of laminated steel. Nothing ever interfered with the output of bar compasses, but for a worrying period, owing
to a serious shortage of steel points fine enough to balance
the magnetized swingers, we were unable to continue
with our better-class models. Fortunately we were not
held up for long. We found an adequate substitute in the
nearest music shop—gramophone needles. We merely cut
the needles down to the requisite length and fitted our
improvised supports in the bottoms of the metal cups
which contained the delicately poised direction-finders.
Thus another obstacle was swept aside, thanks to the
engineer's genius for reducing difficulties to their simplest
terms.

Whenever I look back on my varied experiences as an
inventor, manufacturer and distributor of escape gadgets,
I always recall my visits to the Old Kent Road factory
with affection. The firm, from its two admirable directors
down to its youngest apprentices, was a happy family
concern. There were no bickerings, no meannesses, no
petty jealousies. If one man achieved a spectacular success, the whole community rejoiced. I shall never forget
how proud we all were of George Waterlow when he
finally produced our tiniest compass – only one-eighth of
an inch in diameter. It was a masterpiece of engineering.
One almost needed a magnifying glass to see the needle.

We reserved this particular gem for very special purposes. Later on in the war I despatched many of them to

France to be used by men of the Resistance. It was actually possible to fit such a compass into a carpenter's pencil. I even concealed one inside a phoney gold tooth. And when the Americans entered the war and I noticed that many of them sported large finger rings, I was quick to pounce on yet another hiding-place. Quite a number of reputable Regent Street jewellers fashioned these monstrous rings for us – each with a neatly sliding panel at the back, behind which a compass could be effectively hidden. Fabergé himself never made a prettier piece of trick jewellery.

So much, then, for compasses. They had caused me many more headaches than the escape maps, but at length I was satisfied that our Old Kent Road products were pouring off the assembly line in sufficient numbers for my purpose, which was, of course, to supply every potential prisoner-of-war with the fundamental escape accessories. 'A map, a compass, and food in a concentrated form' had been Johnny Evans's primary requirements. I had still to deal with the food pack, but that was an item I could produce at my leisure. In my opinion, it was far more important to send a man into battle armed with a map and a compass than with a means of subsistence that would in any case be strictly limited. After all, I told myself, an enterprising escaper could always live on the country.

I did not appreciate the falseness of this conception until I had discussed the matter with Johnny Evans in my office one day. 'I can assure you, Clutty, that the escaper's greatest enemy is hunger,' maintained Johnny. 'When a man is starving, he very soon becomes reckless and insensitive. He takes unnecessary risks. He approaches farm buildings and the dogs give him away. He hunts for food in the fields and falls into the hands of brutal peasants, who usually have 'fun' with an escaped prisoner before passing him on to the authorities. Once a man's belly is empty, he makes a hundred and one mistakes – changes his plans, crosses main roads in daylight, throws himself on the mercy of civilians, ventures into villages, steals, uses violence. You can take it from me, Clutty, that you will be doing a great service for the potential escaper if you provide him with something to sustain him on his long trek.'

Forced to admit that there was much wisdom in Johnny Evans's observations, I decided to leave compass production in the hands of the Old Kent Road experts for a while and concentrate on a suitable food pack.

As the Quartermaster's branch was bound to be involved sooner or later, I deemed it politic to discuss my intentions with my boss before taking any drastic action. I persuaded Johnny to come along and help reinforce my arguments, so together we headed for the Metropole Hotel and Room 424. *En route* we dropped in on a colleague who had recently joined our organization. To our surprise, he was standing in front of a wall map of Western Europe, busily employed in moving a row of tiny Union Jacks, which obviously represented our forces in France. We watched until he had fixed the little flags in their new positions – an alarmingly small semi-circle with its two arms touching the French coast.

'It's as good as over, boys,' he informed us sombrely. 'The whole of the BEF is boxed in round Dunkirk. If we don't get them out, there'll be more prisoners than even you can cope with, Clutty.' He ran his finger along the coastline west of Ostend and eyed me significantly. 'All the maps and compasses in the world won't help now. These poor fellows want boats.'

'They'll get them, too!' I flashed back. 'What do you think, Johnny?'

Johnny Evans pursed his lips and shrugged non-committally. He gazed bleakly at the wall map for a moment or two without speaking. Then, his shoulders hunched, he drifted disconsolately doorwards. 'No use going to see Crockatt now,' he muttered as he passed me. 'He won't be interested in food packs just at present. If I were you, Clutty, I'd go ahead and make them – for the men who'll soon be needing them desperately.' Johnny paused at the door, then concluded cryptically, 'I mean the RAF.'

Even as the door closed behind him, I was crossing over to the desk. I knew exactly what Johnny was getting at. I picked up the telephone, listened impatiently to the usual switchboard buzzing, and then asked for the Air Ministry. I proposed to acquaint the junior service with the escape department's modified aims and intentions.

4   Food for Fliers

Shortly after the Dunkirk miracle of deliverance, a most remarkable young officer strode into my office. Such was his determined bearing and assurance that I never dreamed of challenging his presence. He wore a dirty pair of flannel trousers, a blue jersey, and he was carrying, of all things, a top hat. (Later he told me he had taken them off a scarecrow in a Belgian field.) I stared at his outlandish garb, but the intruder seemed in no wise disconcerted. He approached with purposeful strides and addressed me without preamble.

Quietly he announced, 'My name is Embry. Wing-Commander Embry. I understand that you are interested in escapes and escapers.'

I told him I was and then he quickly unfolded the story of his brilliant escape from Occupied France. At the end of his exciting narrative he began to express himself forcibly on the subject of our air policy. His forthright views, backed by a wealth of experience and knowledge, so fascinated me that I suggested he came and had lunch with me at Simpson's. As we walked along, he reviewed the air situation expertly, concluding with an impassioned presentation of the case for night fighter squadrons 'to shoot the b——s out of the sky'.

When, later on, he outlined his proposed policy in the right quarters, his ideas were not only approved but translated into action. Under Basil Embry's capable direction our night fighter defences were quickly forged into a formidable weapon that was destined to cause the *Luftwaffe* many a headache. In less than fifteen years he was to become Sir Basil Embry and an Air Chief Marshal. My own debt to this man of action was considerable, for right from the start he evinced the strongest interest in my work and never failed to give me his wholehearted support. Speed was his watchword. He had scant respect for peacetime methods and 'the usual channels'.

Over an excellent lunch we discussed new and more direct ways of equipping RAF personnel with escape aids. When we parted, I knew I had found an ally on whose courage and tremendous drive I could always count.

Basil Embry was only one of the three hundred thousand and more Allied servicemen brought back by the little ships to fight again. On the debit side of the ledger, almost a quarter of a million men remained behind as prisoners-of-war – men who knew little or nothing of the efforts being made by our organization to encourage and facilitate escapes. They *had* been told that it was their duty to get away if possible, but as far as the BEF formations are concerned, they had gone into the field before our department had become operative. Without maps and compasses and other escape aids, they would have to improvise and fend for themselves until we could tackle their particular problems.

After the fall of France we enjoyed a brief respite before Goering unleashed the full fury of his *Luftwaffe* on London and the Home Counties. The Battle of Britain was on and German bombs began raining down on soldier and civilian alike.

Early in the morning of December 8th, 1940, I received a frantic telephone call from Dick Richards, begging me to drop everything and proceed at once to the factory. There was no mistaking the note of urgency in Dick's voice, so I rushed down to my car and drove round to the factory with all possible speed. Even before I reached the entrance, I could see the ominous clouds of billowing smoke, the attendant fire engines and dozens of firemen training their hoses on the still smouldering ruins.

With heavy heart I picked my way through the broken glass and rubble, almost weeping over the torn and twisted metal scraps of what had formerly been valuable technical instruments. Working my way round a heap of tangled steel girders, I came face to face with George Waterlow and Dick Richards. George was the first to speak.

'What do we do now, Clutty?' he asked, his wan gaze travelling over the devastated area where only yesterday my compasses were being made.

'Put the bloody factory up again!' I said decisively.

'Easier said than done,' was Dick's gloomy comment.

'I don't see that,' I protested. 'After all, it's only a question of getting the labour and new materials.'

'I wish you were right, Clutty. But you're forgetting all the form-filling and controls. We shall need building permits to begin with. Then, it will take months for the local council's plans to be approved. You can imagine how many petty officials will be sent here to inspect the damage before they even start clearing up the mess.' Dick sighed and then concluded, 'I'd like to see old Beaverbrook's face when he hears that his new bomb-sights have gone out of production.'

Dick's mention of Beaverbrook reminded me how that forceful personality had helped me when I had introduced the first 'Movietone News' to England in the pre-war years. I felt that in a crisis such as the one that confronted us, Lord Beaverbrook was probably the one man in England who could be relied on for prompt and constructive action. 'Take me to the nearest 'phone that's in working order,' I bade my two companions.

Wonderingly they conducted me to an office block that had mercifully escaped destruction. A moment or so later they were listening with something approaching awe to the down-to-earth wording of a four-page telegram I dictated, to be sent to Lord Beaverbrook, describing our predicament and requesting his immediate assistance. My trump card, of course, was that only he could prevent a complete break-down in the vital bomb-sight deliveries to the RAF. When I put down the telephone, both George and Dick prophesied that I would be court-martialled.

They opened their eyes next morning when a convoy of lorries drew up outside the blitzed factory. They were loaded with men and materials, and within a few days the job of reconstruction was well under way. In less than a week bomb-sights were again rolling off the assembly lines, and shortly afterwards, my compass makers were operating with redoubled energy in their new surroundings. 'The Beaver' had once more demonstrated his amazing ability as an organizer. Without his intervention, Messrs Blunt's would have been out of the production battle for a long time.

Meanwhile, because France and the Low Countries had been occupied, we had to review our system of priorities. Hitherto we had been distributing our pre-capture escape material to soldiers and airmen alike, but with the Germans in control across the Channel, we had to give first consideration to the RAF. All their sorties in future would be over enemy-held territory. Once beyond the perilously narrow strip of water dividing us from our opponents, all aircraft put out of action by *Flak* or by the *Luftwaffe*, would come down in Nazi-dominated Europe. Pilots, navigators, tail-gunners and air crew forced to bale out would be instantly liable to capture. Our withdrawal from the Continent, therefore, prompted me to divert all supplies of maps and compasses to units of the Royal Air Force.

At the same time I made it my business to provide the

foodpack that Johnny Evans had been advocating for so long. Consultation with Crockatt brought only a stern reminder that in dabbling with foodstuffs I should be poaching on the Quartermaster's preserves, so I decided to act independently. Civilians had co-operated splendidly over my maps and my compasses. I felt confident that they would again rally round and help me produce an emergency ration box.

The first container I tried was the 'flat fifty' cigarette tin. To begin with, it struck me as being the best shape for the job. Secondly, I thought that thousands of such standard sized boxes would be immediately obtainable. When I found that the tin fitted snugly into the breast-pocket of a flier's uniform, I was happy about my choice. I was not quite so happy when I visited Messrs Wills of Bristol to order twenty thousand empties and was told that none were available. One of the directors pointed out apologetically that both tin and cardboard were in very short supply.

A moment's reflection led me to the simplest way out of the *impasse*. 'I'll take twenty thousand *full* tins, then,' I told the startled director.

'But that's a million cigarettes!' he exclaimed.

'That's right,' I agreed. 'And I smoke twenty a day, so I'll have enough for the next hundred and thirty-odd years.' I grinned and then added in a more serious vein, 'But I'm not interested in the cigarettes. I *must* have the containers, though, and what's more, I propose to take delivery today.'

Eventually the deal was concluded and within an hour the first truck-load was rolling along the A-420 towards Chippenham, where it would join the A-4 that would get me to London. Although the director still regarded me in the light of an amiable eccentric, he no longer

doubted the genuineness of our unusual transaction.
I, too, was perfectly satisfied. I knew I could easily
dispose of the cigarettes through forces' welfare channels.
After I had sold them at cost price, my twenty thousand
'flat fifty' tins would have become my property for
nothing. After all, as Barrière so pithily put it, '*Les affaires
sont les affaires.*'

For the next few days I sat at my desk, surrounded by
a miscellaneous assortment of concentrated foods and
other items, packing and unpacking over and over again,
until I felt certain that not a cubic millimetre of space
had been wasted. Squeezed compactly into my small container were twenty-four tablets of malted milk sweets, a
packet of chewing-gum, a tiny saw, a bar of chocolate,
ten benzedrine tablets, a packet of book matches, a simple
compass, a length of thread, a paper map of Germany, a
paper map of Northern France, a roll of adhesive tape, a
bar of special peanut-blended food and six acid drops.
With careful rationing, there was enough sustenance in
the tin to keep a man going for several days.

Proud of my handiwork, I rushed round to show it to
Johnny Evans. He studied the box and its contents for two
or three minutes, congratulated me on a fine piece of
work, and then pricked my complacency by suggesting
that I should start all over again, as I had left out a most
essential article. Dismayed, I asked him to explain.

'Look, Clutty,' said Johnny with a disarming smile,
'this is a jolly good effort, but unfortunately it won't do.
I don't know how you're going to fit it in, but you *must*
include a water-bottle of some sort. All the food is wasted,
if a man has nothing to drink.'

I grumbled and argued for a time, but in my heart of
hearts I knew that Johnny was right. Considerably
deflated, I returned to my office, emptied the cigarette tin

and gazed at it fixedly whilst I concentrated on the problem Johnny had set me. It was only when I ceased to think
of a bottle in terms of glass or metal that I hit on the
obvious solution. By a few simple adjustments, I managed
to pack most of the original items, but in addition I
wedged in two dozen water-purifying tablets and a thin
rubber bottle capable of holding about a quart.

After Johnny Evans had set the seal of his approval on
my Ration Box Mark II, I prepared thousands of similar
packs, bound a strip of adhesive tape round the edges of
each container and issued them to a number of RAF units.
There were no complaints until one day an airman was
forced to bale out over the Channel not far from Dover.
He had succeeded in keeping afloat in his rubber dinghy,
but feeling hungry whilst waiting to be rescued, he had
opened his food pack, only to find the contents ruined
owing to the sea water that had seeped through the
binding material.

Naturally, I ensured that all tins not yet issued were
re-sealed, this time with waterproof tape, but shortly
afterwards I hit on a much better idea than the 'Flat Fifty'
container. A friendly discussion with Laurence Merriam
(now Sir Laurence), the knowledgeable chairman of Halex
Limited – the well-known manufacturers of tooth-brushes
– led to the introduction of a sort of plastic cigar-case,
which was both water-proof and transparent. This was
made in two halves, so that one section slid neatly into
the other. Slightly larger than the cigarette tin, it enabled
me to include a tube of condensed milk. This Mark III
holdall proved a tremendous success and soon became
extremely popular with the young fliers, particularly as
they could see what was inside it.

In my opinion, there was only one snag about our latest
creation. It was still necessary to supply the rubber water

Button-compasses. The American model, shown opened (*center*) and top view (*right*) and the British "fly" button compass, never detected as a fake as the join was made at the back of the button. For some reason American compass-buttons were made with a hinge.

Even cheap collar-studs revealed a compass when the plastic back was cut away.

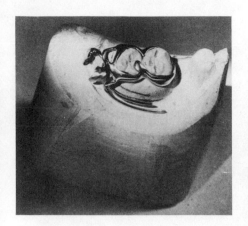 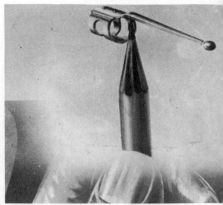

(*Left*) A tiny compass could be concealed within the "jaws" of a gold tooth-frame or brace. (*Right*) Magnetized pencil clips needed only balancing on a pencil.

A shaving brush could conceal currency, maps and a compass. A spool of cotton thread could have a compass hidden within the wooden core, and a pair of dice might open to reveal currency and a compass.

No well-groomed pilot
flew without his razor.
A compass could be
concealed in the end of
the hollow stem, which
held a map, and the
blade was magnetized
and swung to the north
on the end of a thread.

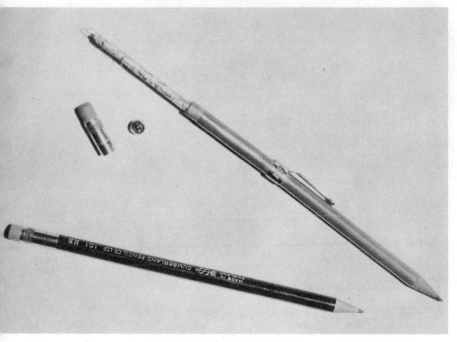

Pencils could be constructed so as to include tiny compasses and rolled-up maps.

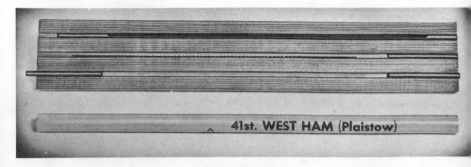

41st. WEST HAM (Plaistow)

Saws concealed in lead pencils were especially constructed on the "fretwork" principle. These were found to be useful in sawing away partitions in prisoners' huts.

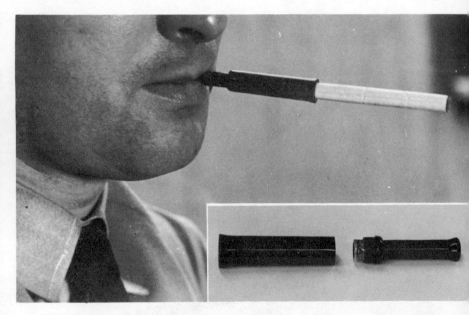

The contracting cigarette-holder-telescope could be used by prisoners to watch their guards at a distance, while seeming to draw on their cigarettes. Each tiny lense was held by a brass ring.

carrier and I strongly disapproved of this bag for a variety
of reasons. I did not fancy the chances of an escaper who
had to depend on an object that was not easy to conceal.
As soon as it was filled with water, the thing was awk-
ward to carry, and in the event of an unexpected
rencontre, there was no disguising its purpose. Besides,
after being folded for any length of time, the rubber
tended to rot at the creases, thus rendering the bag useless.
Then again, rubber was in very short supply and I visualized difficulties later on.

Exactly as I had foreseen, as the war progressed, the
rubber situation became more and more acute. A substitute *had* to be found, so I kept on badgering the plastics
experts at Halex Limited until at last we had the answer
to our prayers. The Mark IV container was made in one
piece, with a shallow neck and screw stopper and with a
large circular aperture in the side. Filled through this
opening, it was made water-tight by fitting a big screw
cap over the hole. One advantage of this model was that
the compass was situated inside the transparent stopper,
and so, in case of emergency, the user could navigate
without having to unpack his box. All he had to do was
to peer into the neck of the container and there was the
magic needle pointing due north. Another improvement
was that it served as its own water-bottle. After transferring the contents to his pockets, an escaper could fill
the plastic box from river or stream, drop in one or two
water-purifying tablets, and there was his *eau potable*. It
could be put down on the ground without fear of the
water running out; its cubic capacity was more than that
of its predecessor; it was curved to the body and consequently could be carried less noticeably in the breast
pocket of a service tunic. The new container was, in fact,
so admirable in every way that it remained unchanged

right through the war. At a later stage, the Americans adopted exactly the same design.

I have already mentioned that Major Crockatt had warned me about interfering with the normal distribution of foodstuffs. From a strictly military point of view I appreciated his attitude, but in so far as my food packs helped men to take evasive action and hindered the Germans from catching them, it seemed to me that they fell within our escape department's terms of reference, and so I obstinately pressed on with my schemes in spite of my Commanding Officer's gloomy prophecies of trouble ahead. With my office looking like a department store, I could only hope that Major Crockatt would have the good sense to leave me to my own devices. That he did so was a tribute to his infinite wisdom and to his tactful recognition of my impatience with rules and regulations.

My first brush with the Ministry of Food occurred when I was experimenting with chocolate. I wanted to produce something that was nourishing, sustaining and wholesome – a blend of pure cream, sugar and cocoa. After a good deal of arguing with the Food Ministry officials, I obtained sufficient quantities of sugar and cocoa, but for a long time the Ministry refused to co-operate with regard to the cream. My repeated inquiries were either ignored or dealt with evasively.

It was a long and bitter campaign, but I hammered away relentlessly at the pettifogging bureaucrats who blindly refused to acknowledge the urgency of my demands. The principle I worked on had been laid down for me by Nelson as far back as 1805. 'It is for each of us in his own sphere to exert himself to the utmost, and not to be nonsensical in saying that I have an order for this or that or the other, where the King's business clearly marks what ought to be done.'

Again and again I hurled myself into the fray, bringing up all the big guns our department could muster, and in the end victory was mine. I discovered that the Ministry's cream stocks were stored at a certain establishment in Wiltshire.

I decided that nothing was to be gained by telephoning or by writing. My only chance of success lay in a personal appeal to the man in charge of such a precious commodity as fresh cream. I *did* toy with the idea of asking if he could see me, but on reflection I thought that shock tactics would probably pay the best dividends.

I drove to the address supplied so reluctantly by the Ministry of Food, ignored the girl at the 'Inquiries' desk and strode unannounced into the director's office. In front of me was a desk of impressive dimensions, and seated behind the desk was a haughty-looking gentleman with a bulging paunch, a flowing moustache and a pair of cold blue eyes that stopped me in my tracks.

'And who the devil are you to come barging in here without an appointment?' he growled. 'Whatever it is you want, I haven't got it. So get out – and stay out!'

'I fancy this will explain everything,' I said, stepping forward and dropping my special identity card on his desk. 'And if that doesn't satisfy you, a call to my Commanding Officer will confirm that I am here on important business.' (I diplomatically refrained from adding that a call to Major Crockatt would more than likely earn me a kick in the pants.)

Anxiously I watched the director pick up my card and examine it thoroughly. When he had finished reading, he took a deep breath, stroked his moustache and barked, 'Well, what is it? Don't beat about the bush. I'm busy.'

'So am I,' I replied, keeping my temper with difficulty. 'And all I want is your help. I need fresh cream.'

'Cream!' The director's eyes bulged incredulously. 'And where the hell do you think I can get cream from in wartime?'

'From a cow,' I ventured. 'Or rather, from lots of cows. Like those.' And I pointed through the window to a pasture where a herd of Shorthorns were placidly grazing.

'We've no cream to spare,' he snapped. 'You're wasting your time and mine. Here you are – and there's the door.'

With a gesture of dismissal, the director handed me my identity card and pretended to busy himself with some papers on his desk. His demeanour was still hostile, but I could have sworn that he was not entirely at ease. Something told me that he was feeling a little ashamed of his unwarrantable rudeness.

'Listen, sir,' I began earnestly. 'This interview started off on the wrong foot, partly because in my eagerness to get results I ignored the formalities, for which I apologize, and partly because of your unco-operative attitude, about which I can do nothing. I could report you to higher authority, of course, but I never have liked asking other people to fight my battles for me. Besides, cooking your goose wouldn't necessarily provide me with fresh cream.'

Out of the corner of my eye I could see that the director had stopped fiddling with his papers and that he was studying me with a new respect, so I made a final bid to win his sympathy. 'Let me put it to you this way, sir,' I went on quickly. 'Suppose you're a young flier, shot down in Occupied France. You've a map and a compass to guide you to safety, but you've nothing to eat. How far do do think you'd get without food?'

'Not far, I imagine,' was the grudging reply. 'But why are you telling me all this?'

'Because part of my job is to make sure that the situation I've just described should not arise.'

'How?'

By way of answer I pulled out of my pocket an empty tube – the type that holds brushless shaving cream. 'Maybe with something like this. Plus a little assistance from you. Take me into your dairy and I'll show you.'

Fascinated in spite of himself, but grumbling for form's sake, the director conducted me to the most magnificent dairy I have ever seen, before or since. We halted near a vat of thick white cream. Picking up a small scoop, I carefully filled the tube from the bottom, pinched the end together with a metal clip and then removed the screw top. I squeezed the tube gently between finger and thumb, and from the nozzle oozed an inch or so of fresh cream.

'Now, sir,' I said, turning to my companion, 'I propose to read the Official Secrets Act to you and afterwards I'll tell you something that is known to very few.' I solemnly intoned the familiar words with telling effect and then continued, 'I've manufactured an emergency food pack for use in the services. It's all part of our plans to encourage evasion and escape. Our biggest headache so far has been making provision for the man who is thirsty. When our medical people informed me that milk or cream would serve admirably if water wasn't available, I hit on this tube idea. One of these included in every ration pack would be a godsend to any man on the run. Our chief customers at the moment, of course, are airmen. I'm sure you'd like to help the RAF, sir.'

The director's next few words told me I had struck the right note. 'Certainly I would,' he declared emphatically. 'You can have all the cream you want on condition you let me deal with you directly, and to a certain extent, unofficially. Don't want to be pestered with inspectors and regulations and all that damned form-filling procedure.'

I assured him gravely that I fully appreciated his sentiments. 'In any case,' I went on, 'my requirements will be surprisingly modest. I'll take deliveries personally or send an accredited representative, and I'll make myself responsible for all payments. I'll also send you a letter from my department that will cover you in the event of bureaucratic meddling. Or better still, refer any Nosey Parkers to me and I'll guarantee they won't worry you again.'

All affability and *bonhomie* now, the Dairy King promised me his full support, and waxing enthusiastic over my tube of fresh cream, insisted on accompanying me to my car. For my part, I was quietly congratulating myself on the skill with which I had handled a tricky situation. I naturally attributed his change of heart to my subtle flattery, to the way in which I had appeared to take him into my confidence, to my casual reference to 'higher authority'. His parting words, however, caused me to think again.

'Best of luck, Mr Hutton,' he said, as I slid into the driver's seat, 'and let's hope the escapers and evaders enjoy my cream. They ought to. It's the best in the world.' He started to walk away, stopped in mid-stride, and delicately fingering his enormous moustache, added with a sly grin, 'Oh yes, I forgot to mention – I have a son in the RAF. He likes cream, too!'

I drove away, pondering on the old tag – 'Every man remembers his own interests.'

Self-interest or not, the Wiltshire dairy-farmer kept me supplied with fresh cream and with various other useful products into the bargain for as long as our escape organization continued to operate. The director and I became firm friends. His son eventually emerged from the war with a distinguished flying record. Not once, I am happy to relate, was he called upon to squeeze his father's cream from one of my unusual containers.

5 Talking of Boots . . .

At this stage in my narrative, the curious reader is probably asking himself who paid for all my maps, silk, compasses, dairy produce and so on. It is obvious that large sums of money were involved; it is equally obvious to anybody who has had dealings with the Treasury that all cash drawn on public funds has to be strictly accounted for, with each item purchased carefully tabulated and the whole story of expenditure supported by bills and vouchers and dockets and what have you. In peacetime such a detailed method of book-keeping is perhaps excusable; in wartime it is preposterous, purposeless and altogether intolerable.

Or so I found it.

Because I was keen to get on with the job, and because I have never required more than five or six hours' sleep out of the twenty-four, I used to devote an average of eighteen hours a day, seven days a week, solely and exclusively to matters appertaining to escape. I firmly believed in the value and importance of my work and consequently I flung myself into it with something approaching fanaticism. I thought only in terms of escapes and evasions. All else, in my estimation, was irrelevant.

It irked me, therefore, whenever I was obliged to justify my frequent demands for financial backing. There were days when the Treasury's cheese-paring attitude almost drove me to revolt. Time and again I had to abandon some vital project or other to answer letters from Civil Servants whose imbecile queries suggested that the writers had not yet realized that a state of emergency existed. During those dark days when German bombs and incendiaries

were raining down on London, these blinkered pen-
pushers were quibbling over pennies and halfpennies.

What really infuriated me were the occasional thinly
veiled accusations that I was perhaps feathering my own
nest on the side. When I was unable to give a detailed
explanation as to how some of my larger bills had been
incurred, I was invariably subjected to a barrage of im-
pertinent and insulting inquiries, some of which implied
that I was guilty of juggling with public funds. The truth
of the matter was that to avoid delays, I very often paid
for urgent stores out of my own pocket, and in the stress
of events I omitted to claim many a legitimate refund.
These periodic nibbles at my own capital left me almost
a thousand pounds the poorer at the end of the war.

Then, one day, after crossing swords with a particularly
obnoxious accountant, I felt so exasperated that I
promptly downed tools and rushed round to the Ministry
of Supply. There I was most sympathetically received by
Sir George Weir, who was in charge of the textile section.
At that first interview I had intended confining my
remarks to silk supplies, with a view to persuading the
Ministry to make itself responsible for my purchases of
that material.

Righteous indignation, however, betrayed me into a
vitriolic denunciation of the whole limping system of
Treasury accounting. Sir George – God bless him! – heard
me out patiently, posed a number of shrewdly pertinent
questions, put forward a few notions of his own, and
assured me that my worries were as good as over. 'Leave
it to me, Hutton,' he said, 'and rest content that something constructive will be done. I shall take up the matter
immediately with the Treasury. I fully agree that the
work you are doing should not be hampered in any way.
It's perfectly plain to me that before long you'll be talking

in thousands of pounds, never mind hundreds. I'll be getting in touch with you.'

Sir George was as good as his word. After a conference
in Portland House in April, 1941, a far-reaching resolution
was approved. The Ministry of Supply and the Treasury
between them would henceforward pay all bills initialled
by me.

From then on, until the escape department closed down,
the Treasury never once haggled over prices, although
some of the items on my bills must have puzzled accountants and auditors. The code names I used for security
reasons were admittedly misleading. Silk maps, for example, were always referred to as 'eggs and bacon', whilst
to those in the know, 'pork sausages' represented paper
maps. But no matter how I labelled my purchases, and no
matter how much I spent, I never again had to bother my
head about financial arrangements. Thanks to Sir George
Weir's magnificent efforts on my behalf, I was able to 'go
the limit' as far as escape aids were concerned. In a single
afternoon, towards the end of 1941, the Treasury gave me
a credit of £150,000!

By August of that year, when I was still operating on
my own, without even the services of a typist, I was able
to report that I had devised, manufactured, packed and
distributed to various combatant units well over one hundred thousand escape aids. These items included maps.
both paper and silk, swinger compasses, stud compasses,
fly-button compasses in pairs, and button compasses.
Owing to pressure of work, I had kept no record of my
ration pack issues, but the number of satisfied customers
must have run into thousands.

It was about this time, too, that my two friends, George
Waterlow and Dick Richards, provided me with yet
another escape gadget. They conceived the idea of mag-

netizing the metal tags of boot-laces, so that they could be removed by the wearer and used as bar compasses. Our list of escapers' accessories was steadily growing.

This successful experiment with the magnetized tags undoubtedly led me to investigate the possibilities of the bootlace as a hiding-place. I had already given some thought to concealing fretsaw blades in articles of clothing, but I had not yet achieved any notable results. I now tried fitting one into a hollow bootlace. Although the introduction of the blade presented no difficulties, its brittleness and rigidity stiffened the lace in an unnatural manner, so I gave up trying and turned to other problems.

A day or two later I happened to be talking to a friend whose father was a brain specialist. Apropos of nothing, I suddenly mentioned that I was searching for a small pliable saw, powerful, yet no thicker than a piece of string. Had he any notion where I should find such a thing?

'What you want,' he said, 'is the kind of saw my old man uses for cutting through people's skulls. It's a flexible length of saw-toothed wire with a loop at each end. To operate it, you put metal bars through the loops and work them as handles. My father says that provided the tension is correct, by employing a steady two-handed movement you can cut through the hardest substance in an incredibly short space of time. A 'Gigli' saw, I believe he calls it.'

'How would a layman get hold of such a professional affair?'

'Buy one, I suppose. They're on sale not far from Oxford Circus, if you're interested. I'll give you the address.'

His curiosity aroused, my friend went on to ask me why I wanted a Gigli saw, but I managed to fob him off with some plausible explanation. I jotted down the name and address of the firm, abruptly took my leave, grabbed the first disengaged taxi I saw and shot round to Oxford Circus. By-passing the usual outliers, I was soon inside the managing director's office, watching a most convincing demonstration of the Gigli saw actually at work. Manipulated exactly as my friend had described, the fine wire bit its way through a metal lug, which was part of a window fitting.

After telling the managing director a little about my business, I offered to buy his entire stock.

'But I've only two dozen,' he protested. 'How many do you really need?'

'To begin with,' I said calmly, 'ten thousand. Subsequent orders may very well be heavier.'

Visibly shaken, the managing director blinked at me bewilderedly. 'Ten thousand Giglis!' He exclaimed. 'You may as well ask for the moon. They're manufactured from a very special steel wire, which is quite unobtainable. Why don't you —'

'How much wire would be required?' I interrupted.

'Not less than a mile.'

'You shall have it within forty-eight hours,' I promised him. 'Any other problems?'

The poor fellow shook his head negatively. As though in a trance, he went over to a wall cupboard and took from it twenty-three six-inch lengths of wire similar to the one he was holding. He made a neat parcel of the tiny bundle and handed it to me. The transaction had so unnerved him that he almost forgot to present me with a bill.

A lightning visit to a Birmingham factory provided me with a mile of the curiously rough wire. I should have liked to have seen the managing director's face at the moment of delivery, but by then I was occupied with another matter. Eminently satisfied that the Gigli saws could be inserted into bootlaces without fear of detection, I had transferred my attention from laces to the boots themselves. Perhaps they, too, could be modified in a manner that would further our escape scheme.

We were naturally interested in the stories of airmen who had been compelled to bale out over Occupied Europe and who had managed to find their way back to this country. Factual accounts of their evasions and clandestine journeys helped us tremendously in the preparation of our pre-capture devices. Many a young flier frankly admitted that he would not have got very far without his map, compass and ration pack. Most of them had only one complaint to make – they were handicapped by their flying boots. In wet weather they became soggy and uncomfortable and tended to slow the wearer down. If it was dry, marching for any distance in the fur-lined boots caused feet and legs to swell and eventually produced raw sores. At all times their distinctive appearance attracted immediate attention, thus ruling out any possibility of movement by day.

With a view to eliminating all these disadvantages, I set about designing an entirely new flying-boot. Fully aware that there would be unpleasant repercussions later, I dashed off to Northampton, called at one of the big boot and shoe factories there and ordered several pairs of flying-boots to be made according to my own specifications. When the manager babbled about the leather shortage, I assured him that supplies would be forthcoming if the boots were a success. Mysterious and not altogether truthful references to my connections with the Ministry of Supply and the War Office convinced him that I was a person of some consequence, so he gave my little job top priority.

When the boots were ready, I showed them to C.-in-C. Bomber Command. He fingered the supple leather approvingly and asked me what was the idea of the strip of webbing running round the boot at ankle level.

By way of answer I extracted a tiny knife blade from the cloth loop at the top of one of the boots and with it I cut through the webbing.

'There you are, sir,' I said, as I separated the two sections. 'The perfect escape boot. Two compasses and a powerful saw in the lace; the bottom part easily detachable to make an ordinary walking shoe; the top half, lined with fur, can be used with the top half of the other boot to provide a warm winter waistcoat.'

'Bomber' Harris was so impressed that he invited a number of pilots from the big air station at Abingdon to come and inspect the boot. Everybody agreed that it was a superb piece of craftsmanship and superior in every way to the suede model issued through normal channels. I gave away the few pairs I had with me and returned to my office to arrange for the factory to go into large-scale production.

Rather foolishly I had given my telephone number to one of the Abingdon pilots. He must have got in touch with friends at bomber stations all over the country, praising the boots and advising them to get their orders in early, for within three days there were inquiries pouring in from every corner of England. I noted down names and locations and promised that all demands would be met as quickly as possible.

There were five thousand pairs in the boot factory's first consignment. As I had received orders far in excess of that number, I had to distribute my wares with wisdom and discretion. I began by supplying the bomber crews, because their work was the most dangerous at that time.

After an astonishingly long and undisturbed spell in the boot trade, an angry screed arrived from the Director-General of Equipment at the Air Ministry. There was no point in panicking, so I waited for the inevitable follow-up letters before I handed over the correspondence to my Commanding Officer. Worded in coldly official language, the complaints all boiled down to the inescapable fact that I had sinned in trying to do the job of the Equipment Branch of the RAF.

Accustomed as he was by that time to my unorthodox methods, Crockatt did not even bother to reprimand me. He merely gave me an old-fashioned look and jerked his thumb doorwards in a gesture with which I was only too familiar. I assumed my penitential expression and gratefully made my escape.

Although – as I discovered later – Crockatt filed away the Equipment Branch's vapourings and conveniently forgot them, the Director-General took no further action. I imagine the bomber squadrons must have put forward such a strong case for the adoption of the Hutton flying-boots that he decided to let my unauthorized issues continue. After all, whatever views he might have held concerning my irregular conduct, he could not shut his eyes to the obvious. My boots were not only better; they were much cheaper.

Then I had another brainwave. Why should we not use the heel of the boot as a cache?

In pursuit of this idea, I consulted with the experts at the Northampton factory and before long we were issuing a special line in flying-boots. After removing some cobbler's wax which had been applied where the heel joined the upper, the wearer could slide back the heel and thus reveal a cavity large enough to hold several silk maps, a compass and a small file. Fortunately, before we had manufactured many models of this type, it was brought to our notice that the sliding heel was difficult to manœuvre when the boot had been exposed to heavy rain. It was hard to push back in order to release the gadgets and still harder to replace. We therefore developed a much more practical affair with a layer of leather along the straight edge of the heel. Underneath this was a cleverly fitted miniature door which could be swung open to remove the equipment and which could afterwards be closed effectively no matter how inclement the weather happened to be. Neat, simple and serviceable, this false heel was a feature of all flying-boots supplied by our escape department from that day forward. It proved very popular amongst pilots generally, and as a hiding-place it was rated very highly by escapers and evaders alike.

With four major escape accessories already in service and a number of other gadgets and devices in the experimental stage, I felt I was justified in asking my Commanding Officer to provide me with a small team of assistants. He told me that he had already applied for an increased establishment. When it came through – and there was no doubt that it *would* come through – I would not only be given all the help I needed; I could also look forward to a spot of promotion. The fact that I had struggled along single-handed under such abnormal conditions had been noted and would eventually be properly recognized. For the time being, it was simply a question of hanging on for at least another few weeks.

I told Major Crockatt bluntly that I was interested neither in promotion nor in dubious decorations. My requirements were merely additional manpower and an office large enough to swing a compass in. I added that my working quarters were so cramped for space that it was easier to squeeze twenty items into a ration pack than it was to introduce one ration pack into the office.

The interview ended with the harassed Crockatt promising to find me alternative premises in which to house my escape material. Before he got round to implementing his promise, however, fate stepped in, this time in the shape of a German bomb which some insensitive *Luftwaffe* pilot actually dropped on the corner of the War Office building. It did little damage, except to morale, but a few days after the incident, the authorities decided that the best answer to Goering lay in immediate evacuation.

As a result of the War Office's dispersion policy, the escape department departed to Beaconsfield, where we moved into a requisitioned country residence standing amongst acres of rolling parkland. I never discovered what part Major Crockatt had played in arranging that we should take over this magnificent mansion. That it was within easy walking distance of his own home might have been pure coincidence. All I know is that I was allocated office accommodation that would have satisfied even Cecil B. de Mille. After my poky War Office box, the panelled chamber in which I was ceremoniously installed was almost frightening in its impressive grandeur. I felt lost in it.

Then, shortly after our arrival, the proposed new establishment was sanctioned. Major Crockatt became Colonel Crockatt, and other promotions, including my own, automatically followed. It was fascinating to watch the show expand. Young officers, NCO's, private soldiers, ATS elements – all converged on Beaconsfield to be fitted into their various niches.

I was beginning to think that my gadget section had been overlooked in all this reorganization, when one morning there was a gentle tap at my office door, and in walked a tall willowy brunette, neat but not particularly

prepossessing in her shapeless khaki uniform. She had one
of those round friendly faces that usually run to dimples,
a nose a shade too broad and I was uncomfortably aware
of a slight cast in her left eye.

She stood just inside the door, favoured me with a
wintry smile and saluted awkwardly. 'I was told to report
to you, sir,' she said. 'I'm your new driver – Jill Warwick.
The Colonel said you would give me my instructions.'

'Did he now? What else did he tell you?'

The girl hesitated for a moment and then blurted out,
'He said that you were mad, sir, and would have to be
humoured!'

Surveying the crazy miscellany of escape equipment
that littered my desk, I chuckled to myself. 'Well, for the
moment,' I said, 'there's nothing for you to do, but you
can – er – humour me in one thing. No more salutes, as
far as I'm concerned. If ever I'm in uniform – and I hope
to God it's not often – I may fling *you* one up, but don't
reciprocate. It's undignified, unnatural and unwomanly. If
you must acknowledge me, just give me a friendly wave.'

And on this improper piece of advice, my first encounter with Jill Warwick was terminated.

6 On Ilkley Moor

Subsequently another driver reported to us for duty. A former porter on the Southern Railway, Private Leary was a six-foot, red-headed cynic who knew all the answers. He proved a valuable asset to my section, where business was not always conducted strictly according to the letter of the law. He was a fast, erratic·driver, but he miraculously managed to avoid accidents. During his leisure hours he devoted himself to the entertainment of any young ladies foolish enough to listen to his cunningly worded arguments in favour of free love. Many a village maiden in the Beaconsfield area fell for Leary's glib patter, frolicked with him for a season and then found herself literally holding the baby.

A day or so after Leary's arrival, I was asked if I had anybody in mind for appointment as my second-in-command. I should have liked to have nominated one or the other of my two sons, Michael and Peter, but neither of them was available. Peter had joined the Australian Army and had recently been wounded in Tobruk; Michael, sunk during convoy work in mid-Atlantic, had been struck on the head by a floating baulk of timber and had not yet been released from hospital. There was another Peter, however, almost equally dear to me, whom I had watched grow up from boyhood into a charming young man with a quick lively mind, an abundance of energy, and a wonderful sense of humour. I refer to Peter Baker, who at that time was learning to be a gunner with an Army Cadet Corps up in Scotland. I could think of nobody better fitted to be my assistant.

The fuss that followed my request for Peter's transfer

could not have been greater had I demanded a complete reorganization of the army. For once, I had gone through the 'usual channels', sending a polite letter to the relevant War Office branch, explaining exactly why I wanted Peter Baker and nobody else. I suggested that he should be given an immediate commission and posted to the escape department forthwith.

I sat back and waited confidently, but Peter failed to put in an appearance. Instead, I received an unpleasantly peremptory summons to visit a fairly high-ranking officer at the War Office. There could be little doubt that something outsize in the way of imperial rockets would shortly be fired in my direction.

As soon as I entered the office of the General who had been deputed to cut me down to size, I was subjected to a scathing commentary on my life, habits, past, present and very uncertain future. His face as red as the tabs on his lapels, his vocabulary choice and extensive, this loud-mouthed Whitehall warrior practically accused me of attempting to sabotage the war effort. 'Good God, man,' he concluded, "you must be fully aware that this youngster is A.1!'

'I am,' I admitted calmly, 'but I also happen to know in which subjects he specialized at school. My show is getting more and more technical. Young Baker has all the qualifications necessary to cope with my really complicated gadgets. Apart from that, the boy's got personality and initiative. Given sufficient training, he'd be able to run the show if I were to crack up. Anyway, I want him – at least for a while.'

'Well, you can't damn well have him!' roared the irate General, thumping the top of his desk by way of emphasis.

'What will you bet?' I demanded sweetly, and without waiting for his reply, I made a hurried exit.

Telling myself that an appeal to Crockatt would get me nowhere, I took the bull by the horns and called upon a certain gentleman in an office not very far away from Downing Street, gave him an appreciation of the situation, hinted that without Peter Baker as my second-in-command, my section of the escape department would more or less cease to function, and finished up with an impassioned plea for the great man's prompt intervention.

My top level appeal did the trick. In less than a week, Peter was commissioned and posted to me. Right from the start he flung himself enthusiastically into our peculiar work, always seeking to improve devices already in production and frequently coming forward with excellent ideas for new gadgets. As my right-hand man, he was kept constantly on the go, but he accepted our overloaded timetable with commendable cheerfulness. I can truthfully state that throughout the whole period of our association together, Peter never once let me down.

It was a sad day for the escape department when eventually Peter was moved overseas into a more active and dangerous field, but none of us was surprised to hear that he had been awarded the Military Cross. It seemed ironic that he should be taken prisoner before the war ended. With his inside knowledge of escape procedure, he must have been a thorn in the flesh of any German camp commandant. One thing is certain. Throughout his captivity, Peter maintained an absolute silence concerning our activities.

I celebrated these more than welcome staff increases by inventing the escape pen. That the ordinary fountain-pen became the escaper's friend was due entirely to my desire to provide my 'customers' with dyes. Before breaking out of a camp, the prisoner had to furnish himself with clothes that resembled those of an average German labourer.

Uniforms could easily be modified, but it was also necessary to change their colour. Dyes in a concentrated form would do the trick; my task was to find a hiding-place for them that would not be suspected by the Germans.

While I was pondering over this question of concealment, I took out my pen, unscrewed the cap and idly began to doodle. I was just trying to decide whether my doodle resembled a man with a beard looking left or a girl with long hair looking right, when suddenly I realized that the answer to my problem lay in my hand at that very moment. My concentrated dye could be introduced into the rubber ink bag of most makes of fountain-pen. Better still, if the rubber tube was to be divided into *three* sections, one could contain a brown dye, another a blue dye, and the third – the one nearest the nib – could be reserved for real ink, so that the pen would behave like all other pens.

After two or three successful experiments, I was satisfied that the bag of dyes would fool the Germans. I was also confident that the pen as a whole would be given only the most cursory of examinations, so I finished up by transforming it into a veritable escaping kit. The filling lever, the clip and the nib were all magnetized and would swing north when suspended on a piece of thread; one of our 'baby' compasses was inside the top of the cap and another lay under the bag of dyes, fitting snugly inside the barrel. There was even enough space below the bag for a few aspirin and benzedrine tablets. And my crowning achievement was to devise a dummy barrel, fractionally larger than the genuine article, so that one of my silk or paper maps could be secreted between the inner and outer cylinders.

I could do no more. My pen could do everything except write under water.

From the pen I naturally turned to the propelling pencil and exploited its possibilities to the full. I also replaced a short length of lead in an ordinary pencil with a strip of magnetized steel of the same size, and so yet another *cache* for compasses was discovered. Lest the Germans should wonder why so many of our men were in possession of new pencils, I employed only old half-used well-bitten stumps for this particular escape aid. I obtained all the dirty, half-chewed pencils I needed by going round a number of schools in the London area and offering to exchange new HB's for bits and pieces that seemed hardly worth sharpening. The gratified youngsters co-operated splendidly, blissfully unaware that they were contributing to a gigantic escape scheme.

Other items we perfected during the first few months at Beaconsfield included a torch that automatically stood upright in the water and emitted the Morse distress signal 'SOS'; a flip-book of successful British bomber raids that I proposed to use for propaganda purposes, and phoney clothing of every description.

My ultimate aim was to smuggle as much escape material as possible into the actual prisoner-of-war camps. It was whilst probing the outer defences that I had occasion to glance through a batch of reports made out by men who had managed to give their captors the slip and return to this country. Some of these escapes and evasions had been performed without any adventitious aids whatsoever, but most of the men on the run had relied on the contrivances issued to them by our escape department. Although it was gratifying to learn that our efforts thus far had not been wasted, I could have kicked myself when I read that there was one very obvious and incalculably useful device that all prisoners longed to possess and that I had done nothing at all about it. I refer, of course, to the miniature wireless set. I started out to rectify this omission without delay.

My first attempts to find a really tiny wireless set proved abortive. When I told the manufacturers that I wanted something that was no larger than a packet of twenty cigarettes, they laughed at my folly. For one thing, there were no valves small enough to operate such an affair as I had visualized; for another, even if sets that size were a possibility, labour could not be spared to produce them.

Then, by pure chance, I bumped into an old friend of mine who was on the British Purchasing Commission. He said he was shortly leaving for Washington to occupy himself with Lease-Lend matters. Acting on a sudden impulse, I begged him to send me, by air, whatever baby wireless sets he could pick up on the open market. I emphasized that the cash side of the transaction would be taken care of by our finance branch.

Weeks later, miniature sets of various types began to trickle into my office. My spirits soared as I studied them, especially the one used by the New York police. This telephone set was no bigger than the normal cigar case and could easily be slipped into the pocket. It was plain to me that the radio experts on our side of the Atlantic had been stalling. My cigarette packet set *could* be made, if only I could find someone to attempt it. But who?

I remembered how, years ago, in connection with a *Daily Mail* publicity stunt, I had bought from my good friend Stanley Mullard fifty of the finest wireless sets ever to have been used in public. If anyone could help me, Mullard was the man. His knowledge of radio was boundless and his temperament was such that the tougher the opposition, the more determined he would be to overcome it. I therefore called on him right away, explained all my difficulties and moodily added that the general consensus of opinion was that the task I had set could not be carried out, not even by the cleverest of wireless wizards.

Mullard laughed me out of my gloom. 'If you can get hold of a few sample valves,' he said, 'from your pal in America, I'll guarantee your midget set can and will be produced, and within the next three months. In the meantime, I'll introduce you to the people who will cheerfully take on the assignment. And what's more, the finished product will be of Rolls Royce quality – a precision job. Grab your hat and come with me.'

Soon afterwards I was sitting in Stanley Mullard's car, wondering where on earth he could be taking me. I shook my head over my own obtuseness when he drew up outside the research laboratories of the GPO. The Government Wireless Experimental Department was the one place I had overlooked. And all the time their workshops were specially designed for solving tricky radio problems, whilst their engineers were capable of tackling the most complicated jobs.

After all the rebuffs I had received from the big electrical organizations, it was heart-warming to be greeted with unfeigned enthusiasm by the members of the vast Government concern. The Chief Engineer, Mr Doust, quickly dispelled my nervous fears that the scientists employed there would already be so weighed down with other war commitments that they would have no time to deal with my relatively unimportant business. He told me that, on the contrary, they had not yet been approached by any of the three services and that they would be only too delighted to tackle something that lay outside the daily routine. He did not propose to ask *why* I wanted such tiny sets. It was not even necessary to state in which countries they would be operating. All he needed to know was the approximate distance in miles over which they would be expected to receive transmissions.

'Let us have a good supply of the valves as soon as possible,' were his parting words, 'and then leave the rest to us. I'll get in touch with you if we strike lucky.'

That same evening I rang up my friend in America and implored his immediate assistance. He responded magnificently, for in less than a week a large parcel, carried by bomber from Washington, was delivered at my office. It contained one thousand of the precious valves, each no larger than a pea-nut. I rushed round to the GPO laboratories and handed them over.

After that, began a nerve-racking period of waiting, which lasted for almost three months. Then, one morning the 'phone rang. Could I call round at the Government Wireless Experimental Department without delay?

On my arrival half an hour later, Mr Doust greeted me non-committally and invited me to lunch. To all my questions about the wireless set he gave evasive replies, recommending patience and hinting vaguely that some progress had been made. When we had finished our meal, he took me on a conducted tour of the huge plant and introduced me to each scientist we met. All the time I was smouldering with disappointment and frustration, but worse was to come.

He took me into his office and produced for my benefit various sample sets. Each would have fitted into a cigarette packet, but every one, I was told regretfully, had a technical fault that rendered it unsatisfactory for the purpose I had envisaged. The GPO expert went into each defect at length in a scientific jargon that served only to increase my irritation.

Convinced in the end that the whole project was a failure, I rudely interrupted a particularly wordy apologia, and mumbling insincere thanks for all his trouble, I moved towards the door. Evidently that was the cue for my host to step across to a cupboard, to haul out a large parcel about three feet square and to deposit it on his desk.

'Open that,' he bade me laconically.

When I had removed the brown paper, I found a great cardboard box. Inside it was a smaller package, which I unwrapped at once, only to discover another cardboard box containing an even smaller packet. I persevered in this manner at least a dozen times until I reached the heart of the mystery – a cubical carton with six-inch sides. I lifted the lid. Within, nestling in a layer of cotton wool, lay the tray of a cigarette packet.

Inside the tray was a midget wireless set.

Mr Doust, grinning at my astonishment, carefully picked up this tiny tribute to the radio engineer's skill and plugged it into the socket of his desk lamp. He next un-wound a coil of very fine wire that was tucked into the back of the set. On the end of the wire was the smallest earphone I had ever seen. He gave the valves time to warm up and then invited me to listen. I could distinctly hear the raucous voice of an American announcing a pro-gramme of music.

'It sounds like New York!' I gasped.

'It *is* New York,' was the astounding reply. 'What do you think of the range?'

'It's staggering. I never expected anything as good as this.' I fingered the delicately fashioned instrument lovingly. 'Is this the only one?'

'Oh no. We've already manufactured quite a number. They're all parcelled up for you to take when you go. And you'll notice there are no knobs and only one simple switch.'

'But how do you tune it?'

'With a screw-driver,' he replied. 'And take a look at the foolproof aerial and earth connections – a wire mattress and a water pipe are all you need. You'll also be pleased to hear that this type of set will work on any electric supply likely to be used in Europe.' He strolled across to another cupboard, opened it and eyed me slyly. 'You'll probably be interested in this gadget. You didn't ask for it, but while we were about it, we thought we might as well do the job properly. It has exactly the same range as the receiver.'

He showed me a baby transmitting set that took my breath away.

As happy as a child with an abundance of Christmas presents, I transported my new toys back to my head-quarters. For once, I did not charge in on my senior officers to demonstrate my treasures. I preferred to lie low for a while and think over the best use to which receiver and transmitter could be put. I was unable, how-ever, to resist the temptation to try them out.

Surreptitiously I built up a small wireless station in my office. The only installation I could not keep under cover was the aerial, which I erected in a tall tree in the grounds. I gave it out that I was trying to improve reception on my ordinary set. Then, after instructing Peter in the art of transmitting and receiving, and warning him that, as radio messages were strictly monitored by the Navy, we should have to operate with circumspection, early one morning I carefully packed the twin midgets, slung a pair of step-ladders into the back of my car, sent for Jill Warwick and invited her to drive me north.

The girl eyed me blankly. North, she hinted delicately, was rather vague. Could I be a little more specific?

Impatiently I consulted an ancient AA Handbook. 'Jot these names down,' I bade her. 'We'll make for Ware, to

begin with. Then come Royston, Huntingdon, Stamford
and Grantham. We'll have lunch there, at the "George".
Next we have Newark-on-Trent, Retford, Bawtry, Don-
caster, York. We'd better stay the night in York and then
we'll be fresh for the following day's manœuvres. On the
Yorkshire moors. Have you got all that?'

In my excitement I had rattled off the place names at
such a rate that my bewildered driver had not even had
time to find paper and pencil. Intolerant of delay, I scrib-
bled the directions on the back of an envelope, paying
little attention to the girl's apologies. 'Our line of march,'
I said, as I thrust the scrap of paper into her hand. 'Don't
worry if you stray off the route. I'll soon get you back on
to it.'

I was quite taken aback when she suddenly snapped at
me, 'I can read sign-posts, thank you very much.'

'So can anybody,' I replied drily, 'if the sign-posts are
there. You're forgetting that most of them have been removed with a view to baffling German parachutists. That's
why I propose to act as navigator. I'm a nervous passenger,
especially with a woman driver, so don't take any stupid
risks. Let me know when you're feeling tired and we'll
stop for a coffee.'

She opened the car door, waited until I was comfortably
installed, slammed the door with unnecessary vigour, and
climbing into the driver's seat, remarked as we moved off,
'Everybody's in such a hurry here. I don't like to be
rushed.'

'Oh, you'll get used to us,' I said cheerfully. 'We just
like to keep up with the enemy. The Germans are in a
hurry, too, you know. We can't afford to let them steal a
march on us. God knows it's taken us long enough to get
into our stride.'

We then drove along in silence as far as Ware. Jill's

eyes were fixed on the road ahead; I studied her profile
covertly from time to time. I could see she was still brooding over my implied criticism and the fact that I had not
allowed her sufficient time to note down our intinerary.
When she took the wrong turning after reaching the
centre of Ware, I was privately delighted.

A fortifying lunch at Grantham sustained us admirably
on the run to York. My intention on arrival had been to
book a couple of rooms at the Royal Station Hotel, but
my driver insisted on finding her own accommodation.
Finally, she allowed me to fix her up at Butts Close in Tad-
caster Road. I instructed her to pick me up at nine next
day and left her to her own devices.

On the following morning, shortly after nine, we drove
out of the city and were soon cruising through Wetherby,
bound for Ilkley Moor. At last, on a secluded stretch of
road on the outskirts of the town, we began our experiments. Aided by the ladder and a skeleton key, I removed
the globe from a nearby lamp standard, detached the light
bulb and plugged in.

Everything worked perfectly. Within a minute I was in
direct communication with my headquarters office. Peter
and I exchanged greetings and various messages and then
signed off. We moved on to a different area and repeated
our performance with the same success. For several days
we dodged about, testing the sets in a dozen localities in
Yorkshire. Everywhere we went, transmission and reception were excellent.

With every day that passed, Jill's interest in my unorthodox activities increased. She was as thrilled about
the midget radio sets as I was. Then, one afternoon, after
an unusually lengthy discussion with Peter, a police car
suddenly appeared, drew up smoothly not far away, and
from it stepped two police officers. They ambled leisurely

towards us and sat down on the grass. Each pulled a packet of sandwiches from his pocket and began to chew ruminatively, all the time keeping us under furtive surveillance. At last one of them spoke. He chatted inconsequentially about the weather and the war situation. Then he demanded point-blank, 'And what exactly are you doing in this area, sir?'

'Resting,' I replied unhesitatingly. 'We're on our way to London.'

Between the two officers flashed a momentary glance that I could not interpret. I was asked to show my identity card. Both men were punctiliously polite, gravely examining the civilian document I showed them and returning it with apologetic grins. 'Oddly enough,' one remarked, 'we are searching for a War Office gentleman with exactly the same name as yours. Investigations suggest that he has been illegally jamming certain service transmissions.' He eyed me innocently. 'I don't suppose you can help us, sir?'

I could see at a glance that it would be a waste of time to continue to bluff it out, so I admitted that I was the person they were looking for. Courteously we were invited to tag along behind the police car as far as Leeds. We obediently played follow-my-leader – doubtless closely watched in the squad car's driving mirror – until we were waved to a standstill in front of a large forbidding-looking building. It was the police station. We were escorted inside and there we were shown into the presence of the man who had been instrumental in tracking us down. He was then a colonel, but before the war he had been employed by the BBC and we had been close friends. He told me with a smile that he had been on our trail for five days. With mock severity he demanded what the devil we had been up to.

Naturally, I gave him a full and truthful account of our manœuvres, and the Colonel assured me that as far as he was concerned, the matter was closed. In tones not entirely friendly he added that I could consider myself lucky, for any case he dealt with finished up normally with a prosecution. When he jokingly advised me to keep off the air in future, I knew he meant what he said.

Jill drove me back to our country residence and on the following day Peter and I dismantled the aerial. The miraculous sets were stowed away in what I had hope-fully called our 'Pending' cupboard, to stay there, as I then thought, until the cessation of hostilities. I remember feeling positively murderous about the criminal waste of such potentially valuable war material. A week later, however, there was a new and unexpected development. Two officers from one of our very 'hush-hush' branches came to see me. They had heard of my long-range minia-ture sets, they said, and would like to examine them. I passed the request on to my senior officers, giving them a brief but not wholly factual résumé of the events that had led up to the inquiry. I was ordered peremptorily to co-operate with my visitors in every way.

And that was the last I ever saw of the cigarette packet radios, for after they had carried out an initial test, the two officers appropriated the complete stock for use in a special organization. It was, I suppose, gratifying to know that all our time and trouble had not been expended in vain. Besides, the escape department was handling in those days such a rich variety of gadgets that we could afford to be generous.

My staff had increased, but supplies of escape gadgets of every kind were flowing into our Beaconsfield offices at such a rate that it was evident we were approaching saturation-point. The food pack in particular was a continual source of worry. Every plastic container had to be filled entirely by hand according to a carefully worked-out system. The slightest departure from our standard procedure meant that something would have to be omitted through lack of space. This necessity for strict conformity to pattern slowed down work on the ration boxes considerably. Either I had to employ outside help or we should quickly find ourselves snowed under with orders we could never hope to meet.

In desperation I sought assistance from the WVS in a nearby village. The response was immediate. A lady, rejoicing in the singular name of Mrs Bote – benevolent, horse-faced and positively quivering with surplus energy – called to inform me that she proposed to start packing for us just as soon as I could arrange for the empty hold-alls and the concentrated food and so on to be delivered to her house. She did not ask if we could use her services. Mrs Bote was not the sort of woman to offer aid. She simply announced a line of action and pursued it without counting the cost.

In my innocence I blessed the indefatigable Mrs Bote, for the good lady not only transformed her house into a small factory; she also started off by putting in an eighteen-hour working day on my behalf. I really thought I had found a treasure when I went round on a tour of inspection. Mrs Bote's nimble fingers moved like lightning, lifting, poking, prodding, tapping, and there, in record time was the plastic box, loaded and ready for issue. With all my practice, I could not have done it either so meticulously or so expeditiously. I stayed for an hour or so, marvelling at her output, and departed fully confident that we could safely leave the preparation of the emergency pack in the capable hands of our new assistant.

But, alas for all my hopes. One day, a visitor – tall, smartly dressed, gentlemanly – strolled into my office, showed me his credentials, said he was closely connected with MI 5 and asked me if I knew a lady called Mrs Bote.

'I certainly do,' I enthused, 'and don't you do anything to upset her. I can vouch for her all right. She's working for this department, and what's more, we couldn't get on without her. Absolutely indispensable. A pearl. Worth her weight in gold.'

'I don't doubt it for a moment, sir,' was the detective's dry comment. 'She's also fond of a glass of stout, and we have it on good authority that she's been in the village pub for the last three nights telling everybody at the bar the type of work she's doing for you. Moreover, she's described the contents of the special parcels she's making up and revealed how many a day are being distributed to the RAF. She may be all you say about her, sir, but she's a bad security risk.'

I tried to persuade myself and the man from MI 5 that the items in the packs were not particularly secret. It was logical to suppose that my plastic box had fallen into the hands of the enemy long ago, that everything inside it had been examined *au fond*, and that somewhere in Germany an organization similar to ours was manufacturing the same sort of thing for their fliers. Unfortunately, that was not the point, as my visitor was quick to stress. Mrs Bote's real crime lay in disclosing our distribution figures. An astute German spy would be able to draw many useful deductions from such numbers.

Under the circumstances I had to admit that Mrs Bote ought never to have been employed by the escape department in the first place. I expressed my gratitude for the warning and promised that no further leakages would occur.

So that same evening, whilst Mrs Bote was holding court in the private bar of the 'Red Lion', a tiny procession of army vehicles drew up outside her house in the village. I was leading the convoy in our Austin Utility, and behind me came two fifteen-hundredweight trucks, driven by Privates Leary and Warwick. Under the curious eyes of the villagers, Leary 'effected an entrance' by means of a badly fastened window and opened the front door. The three of us then removed every scrap of material even remotely connected with the job Mrs Bote had been doing with such speed and efficiency.

I often wonder how she reacted when she returned home, mellowed by a convivial evening, and found all our stuff gone. The fact that she registered no complaint about our nocturnal raid suggested to me that she was uncomfortably aware of her public house indiscretions.

When I informed the detective that we had dispensed with Mrs Bote's services, he expressed himself as satisfied. I shall always remember his final remarks as he left my office. 'And if you think of employing civilians again, sir, I suggest that you have them vetted very carefully before you sign them on. Mind you, I'm surprised that you made use of Mrs Bote. But then, perhaps you don't know any German?'

'It so happens,' I said stiffly, 'that I have a good knowledge of German.'

'Then maybe you've forgotten, sir, that *Bote* is a good

German word.' He crossed over to the door, paused there with his hand on the knob and concluded blandly, 'I believe it means "Messenger"!'

He flung up a mocking salute and was gone, leaving me to curse my own obtuseness. Happily, shortly after the detective's departure, a telephone from my Commanding Officer helped restore my shattered morale. In view of the heavy demands for my gadgets, Colonel Crockatt was pleased to inform me, he was sending along a couple of ATS girls to help me out. He had heard, he added with a chuckle, that our dear friend, Mrs Bote, had sent in her notice . . .

This was excellent news. With two assistants taking care of store-keeping, packing and the minimum of accountancy we bothered about, Peter and I could give our minds to more important matters. And the most important matter of all, as far as we were concerned, was undoubtedly Operation Post-Box.

But before giving a detailed account of what must have been the most impudent of the war's back-room efforts, it is necessary to examine the situation that existed prior to the introduction of our new scheme. To appreciate fully the significance of our next move, the reader must consider for a moment the problems of the man behind the wire, what we had done for him so far, and what we proposed to do for him in the immediate future.

I have already made it clear that most of the prisoners taken up to and including the Dunkirk débâcle marched into captivity bearing practically nothing in the way of escape aids and devices. Possibly a few had their own compasses; a handful might have been in possession of maps; here and there men from the technical arms might very well have been carrying wire-cutters and other handy tools. How many of these items escaped the preliminary

searches we cannot hope to estimate. We can rest assured
that only a negligible quantity got past the final camp
screening.

This lack of material equipment, if we are to accept
the evidence contained in the hundreds of escape books
that emerged after the war, did not deter men who had
the courage, energy and initiative to 'make their own
arrangements'. They had neither maps nor compasses, but
they had plenty of ingenuity and the ability to improvise.
They had something else, too, without which no escaper
could achieve success – sheer 'guts', that indefinable
quality comprising endurance, will-power, fortitude,
patience and a dozen other virtues. And so, without our
connivance, they broke out of prison, some to be interned
in neutral countries, some to get back to the United
Kingdom, and some, alas, to be recaptured and flung back
in gaol.

Escaped prisoners-of-war were always carefully interrogated when they returned to this country. The reports
concerning their preparations, their methods of escape,
their subsequent adventures before reaching safety, all
these were made available for us to study. From them we
learned a good deal that encouraged and helped us in our
work. There were times when escapers had managed to
get hold of some of our gadgets, usually from captured
airmen or from soldiers and agents picked up whilst on
special missions. In short, a little of our equipment had
already infiltrated into the camps.

Now, my aim, right from the start of my association
with the escape department, had always been to discover
a foolproof system for introducing my 'toys' into the
camps themselves. After all, I reasoned, every man behind the wire was a potential escaper, and it was up to us
to make provision for each and every one of them. Escape

accessories, therefore, would have to be delivered, not in twos and threes, but in thousands. To arrange for the odd map and compass to be smuggled to particular prisoners was one thing; to initiate and maintain a steady flow of *all* our devices was another. No wonder I had passed many a sleepless night wrestling with the problem.

But at last I found the solution.

I began by concentrating on clothing. I had to provide would-be escapers with materials from which they could improvise either civilian suits or German service uniforms. To hoodwink the enemy, I arranged for a special RAF pamphlet to be published, announcing that a new mess dress would in future be worn by all personnel as and when supplies became available. This would enable me, when the time was ripe, to furnish captured airmen with outfits that could easily be converted into *Luftwaffe* dress.

With the aid of the Wool Association, we saw to it that the correct cloth was employed. Then, attractive wire facings had to be included, so we simply used suitable lengths of wire to bind up our parcels. The prisoners, we knew, had learnt to fashion their own Iron Crosses, but we thought it would help if we sent them packets of handkerchiefs tied up with strips of black and white material, from which the right ribbons could be made. Our agents across the Channel managed to smuggle out rolls of German leather, which served admirably for the manufacture of *Luftwaffe* boots.

We now prepared thousands of bundles of clothing, most of it being perfectly normal wearing apparel, such as socks, shoes, slippers, dressing-gowns, pants, vests and so on. We usually included, too, such creature comforts as blankets and sheets, working on the assumption that they could be cut up, transformed into civilian jackets, trousers and overcoats, and treated with the dyes I have already mentioned.

Blankets, we gathered, could be converted by the camp tailors into excellent civilian suits. We conducted tests on an abundance of cloths before we finally selected one that was convincing both as a blanket and also when made into a suit. Nor did we lose sight of the fact that thanks to the blockade, the Germans were living in a world where nearly everything was *ersatz*. If a prisoner was to pass himself off successfully as a German civilian in those days, he had to look positively shabby!

We had the clothing and we had the escape aids. My next task was to think out a reliable system of delivery. I had to smuggle the stuff into the camps in a manner that would not arouse enemy suspicions. I also had to evolve a plan whereby the various camp escape committees would know exactly where my bits and pieces were hidden. Finally, whatever method I employed, it would have to be something quite different from the two legitimate supply channels – Red Cross parcels and the monthly personal packages that prisoners-of-war were allowed to receive from their friends and relatives at home. I could not afford to ignore the provisions of the Geneva Convention and I felt that it would have been unfair to have taken advantage of what was, after all, merely a concession. I had no doubt that if the Germans discovered an illegal item in a 'family' parcel, they would have no compunction about withdrawing the privilege altogether. More important still, I had no intention of advertising my nefarious activities.

I must make it absolutely clear that I was never tempted to interfere with Red Cross parcels. All the same I *did* go as far as studying their contents, if only from an academic angle. It was the presence of these items in my office that led to an unforgettable interview with the greatest VIP of them all. Accidentally discovered during an official visit, this stuff that only the Red Cross was supposed to handle was immediately recognized for what it was and I was informed coldly that I should have to explain my actions to higher authority.

I realized how high authority could go when I was visited soon afterwards by a stern-looking elderly gentleman, who was smoking a cigar. 'So you're the fellow who is infringing Red Cross regulations?' he barked at me.

'I'm doing nothing of the sort, sir,' I stoutly maintained.

'Good,' he grunted. 'Always remember that at the end of this war we want to be in a position to say that we fought and won it fairly. I think you're trying to go much too quickly. Reconcile yourself to the fact that it takes us four years to attain victory. In the first year we have to sell the war to the public; in the second we are busy jigging and tooling for the newest weapons; in the third supplies come pouring in; and in the fourth we press buttons everywhere and the enemy has a most unpleasant time. So cultivate patience and – keep your hands clean.'

He waved his cigar at me, and was gone.

I therefore decided to make use of a system that transgressed no written regulations, and which, at the same time, offered a wide field for concealment. We would hide our escape aids in parcels containing games, sports equipment, musical instruments, books and articles of clothing. We knew that these voluntary gifts, designed for the comfort and entertainment of the prisoners, were flooding the camps from hundreds of sources – local associations, WVS, church organizations, sports firms, multiple stores and what have you. There was no valid reason why we should not take cover behind this multiplicity of well-

wishers. I was confident that the methodical Germans had
compiled detailed lists of the donors of these goods, but it
was doubtful if they took any further action in respect of
such seemingly innocent bundles. We were well aware
that the men's personal parcels were subjected to very
thorough searches. It was our guess that only a small
percentage of the general welfare miscellany received anything more than a perfunctory examination. It was a risk
worth taking.

The next move was to establish a number of fictitious
organizations up and down the country. For this purpose
we selected likely addresses – blitzed buildings being ideal
for obvious reasons. Then a printer friend of mine under-
took the design of suitable letter headings, which were
littered with quotations that we hoped would act both as
clues and as an inspiration to the prisoners. One obvious
quotation was from St Matthew, Chapter 7 : 'Ask and it
shall be given you; seek and ye shall find; knock and it
shall be opened unto you.' Arrangements were made for
the diversion of telephone calls, and for the redirection
of any mail. We did have one extremely persistent
correspondent, however, who caused us a certain amount
of embarrassment. She was an old lady, living in the country, whose grandson had written to her from Germany
describing enthusiastically the wonderful parcel he had
received from one of our organizations. She wrote at
length to our 'Miss Mappin', thanking us effusively and
enclosing a cheque for fifty pounds to help provide more
parcels for prisoners. Naturally, I returned the cheque,
telling her politely in my covering letter that the Fund
was not in need of financial assistance and suggesting that
she should send the money to some less prosperous
organization.

A few days later the cheque was back again. She had

sent us the fifty pounds, she stated, because her grandson had specifically urged her to do so. Would we please retain it this time and spend it as we thought fit. There must be *something* we could buy for 'the brave boys in the camps'. She herself, she proudly informed us, had started to knit a balaclava, which she would post to us at a later date. On her next visit to London, she proposed to pop round to express her gratitude personally.

There was only one course left open to me. That same day I went down to the village where the old lady lived, called at her home and let her into at least a part of our secret. After a good deal of friendly argument, she reluctantly took back her much-travelled cheque. Then, looking extremely determined, she sat down at her desk and filled in another cheque right under my very nose. 'And not even General Montgomery can interfere with this one,' she said resolutely. 'If I can't give my money to your organization, I can at least help these dear people.'

She showed me the cheque. It was made out for one hundred pounds and the payee was the International Red Cross.

One of the most amusing of my creations was the donor of large numbers of books to prisoners of war. Our work consisted of tearing off the covers and rebinding, with maps or appropriate foreign currency hidden beneath the new endpapers. A letter went with each parcel from the donor, on the following lines:

Dear Friend,

I am sure you will be sorry to hear that my beautiful vicarage was bombed a month ago by the enemy. Everything was destroyed except my library. As my wife and I feel that it will be some considerable time before we have another home of our own, we have decided that little purpose would be served by putting the books into storage. We are therefore sending them out to the prisoner-of-war camps, hoping that they will do something to sustain the morale of those who, like yourself, are enduring Babylonish captivity.

Please let me know that you have received this parcel safely, and that you are one of those who believe, with Andrew Lang, in

The Love of Books, the Golden Key
That opens the Enchanted Door.

Yours most sincerely,
_____

We sent out the book bundles to the camps in large numbers before the Germans realized that the kind old clergyman had supplied scores of prisoners with Golden Keys that had indeed opened enchanted doors. It was a sad moment when we had to admit that he could no longer be of any use to us.

In our kind of work we always assumed that the enemy was as smart as we were. We argued that if, over a period, he was confronted with identical wrapping papers and string from places as geographically apart as, say, Sheffield, Chester, Gloucester and Maidstone, he would begin to suspect that our little bands of philanthropists were not entirely above board. Consequently we acquired large stocks of brown paper and cord of varying qualities. We also bought suitably dated copies of local newspapers to use as internal packing to protect the separate articles inside each bulk consignment. If we were sending out a selection of indoor games from Liverpool, we would go to the trouble of first wrapping the Ludo board and counters, the box of dominoes, the set of chess men, the packs of cards, the carton containing the Blow Football apparatus, the dart board and darts in sheets torn from the *Liverpool Echo*. The *Manchester Guardian*, the *Oxford Mail*, the *Staffordshire Sentinel*, the *Dover Express*, the *Birmingham Post*, the *Evening Standard* – these and dozens of other papers, used as padding, all helped to establish our *bona fides*.

As a further precaution, when we were despatching indoor games, we saw to it that they varied in make-up from locality to locality. The snakes and ladders on the board sent from Bristol writhed and inclined in a pattern different from that designed on the board from Norwich. Table-tennis bats from Crewe had rubberized surfaces; those from York were in plain wood. Playing cards from Canterbury had a coloured picture of the Cathedral on their backs, whilst the famous Pavilion adorned the backs of cards sent from Brighton.

To start off with, we enclosed nothing 'tricky' in our consignments. They were all legitimate bundles of items of entertainment that the Germans could not possibly take exception to. The recipients – chosen usually at random from available prisoner-of-war lists – were in camps all over Germany. As we wanted to know if our parcels were reaching their destinations, we enclosed with each package a printed card of acknowledgment on which the contents were enumerated. All the prisoner had to do was to tick off each article as received and return the card, which was, incidentally, one-sixteenth of an inch bigger all round than the one used by the Red Cross and could thus be quickly sorted out by the censors for forwarding direct to us.

The waiting period seemed interminable. We grew more and more depressed, telling ourselves gloomily that the Jerries had confiscated the lot and we should hear no more about the matter. But we were wrong. Three months after we had shipped the first cargo, a solitary card arrived. Within a few days others followed thick and fast. Our stuff was getting through!

Then came the second and vital phase of our scheme. The despatch of bundles that were not all legitimate. Somewhere, in a very small percentage of the total load, were concealed our escape devices. We employed a variety of hiding-places, carving out secret caches in the handles of table-tennis bats, in chess men and in the wooden frame of the board, in dominoes, in Indian clubs, in skittles, in cricket balls, in darts and in dart boards, in drum sticks and in the hammers of dulcimers.

I need hardly say that these plans of mine were greeted on all sides with complete scepticism. Even Major Crockatt said to me as the first thirteen *loaded* parcels were sent, 'They will never get through in one hundred years.' But once again, after the usual delay, we heard that everything, including the fake material, had been delivered. We had our entrée to the camps.

8 'F' For Freddie

On our side of the Channel, then, all was well. But what was happening at the receiving end – in the camps themselves? To whom were our entertainment items being delivered and what provisions were being made to guard the gadgets against discovery by the German gaolers? How was it possible to keep such a mass of material from prying eyes in a very much restricted area, where places of concealment were few and organized searches were frequent?

Communications at top level are not my concern in this volume, so I shall not enlarge on the means by which a constant interchange of information was maintained between the prisoner-of-war camps and our Intelligence branch throughout the whole of the war. It is sufficient to say that one officer in each camp knew precisely what stuff had been forwarded, how it was disguised and in whose possession it ought to be. He was able to send messages concerning escapes effected, escapes about to be launched, and escapes still in the planning stage. He was even able to furnish a list of urgent requirements, such as wire-cutters, files, knife blades, inks, dyes, chalks, soap, glue, diamonds (for removing glass window panes), piano wire, everything.

The position behind the wire, then, was this. In any camp at any given time would be thousands of Allied prisoners. All shared the dream of getting back to the outside world, but only a handful felt the urge to make of that dream a tangible reality. These few would be passing through the normal pre-escape phase – plotting, forging, digging, dyeing, reconnoitring, hoarding – leading a fur-

tive under-cover existence that would set them apart from
their fellows. Also in the same camp would be a large
number of prisoners who, to their surprise and gratifica-
tion, had received in the past various unexpected packages
from some equally unexpected and curious organizations.

Then, one day, a prisoner – let us call him Smith –
speaks to the officer in charge of escapes. He outlines his
escape plan, describes his preparations, mentions the
equipment he has begged, borrowed or stolen, and displays
the spurious documentation he proposes to use.

The other officer says, 'Yes, Smith, I think it ought to
work. You'll need the new railway pass, but I'll arrange
that for you. Now, you say you intend making for the
Swiss frontier. Have you got a map or a compass?'

Smith shakes his head regretfully. With some diffidence
he propounds his theory that the surest guides are the sun
and the stars and a quick intelligence. Yes, he would very
much prefer map and compass, but, *faute de mieux*, he
is going to rely on his native wit, plus a fluent knowledge
of German.

'I may be able to help you,' is the officer's non-com-
mittal comment. 'I suggest you defer your exit until
Friday. I happen to know it's the Camp Commandant's
birthday. He's sure to have a party for the officers, so the
guards will be taking things easy that night. Come and see
me on Thursday afternoon for a final briefing.' A few
minutes later the Escape Officer chats to two other officers.
Quite casually he steers the conversation round to the
subject of letters and gift parcels. 'I believe that you,
Jones, received a set of darts the other day and that you,
Robinson, were lucky enough to get a chess set?'

Both men, flattered by the officer's obvious interest in
their welfare, admit that he is right, though they are
somewhat mystified that he should know the precise con-

tents of their parcels. They are even more at sea when he asks them to fetch the darts and chess men along to his hut. By the time they have delivered the articles and have left them with the officer, receiving what appear to be identical darts and chess pieces in return, they conclude that they are dealing with an eccentric and are clearly relieved when the interview is over.

As soon as he is alone, the officer peers closely at the three darts, then picks one up, and holding the metal band that encircles the wooden shaft, he twists the body of the dart in a clockwise direction. It unscrews without much difficulty, and there, inside the hollow chamber thus revealed, protected by cotton wool, is a compass no bigger than the old-fashioned threepenny bit.

He next takes up the two black castles from the chess set. He tries first one, and then the other. The crenellated turret of the second castle also unscrews, and that too has a left-hand thread. With an exclamation of satisfaction, the officer fishes from a neatly hollowed cavity a compressed ball of silk and smoothes it out on his table top. It is a seven-coloured map of Germany.

When Smith makes his trip on Friday night, while the camp officers are roistering in the Commandant's quarters, and the sentries are relaxing with a bottle or two of schnapps, he will have in his pocket the map and compass that may guide him to Switzerland. Good luck to him!

Such was the scheme in all its simplicity. The beauty of it was that our escaper never knew that he had probably thrown a double top with the dart that had contained his compass, and that when he had castled on the King's side in his last chess match with Robinson, his fingers had been within a sixteenth of an inch of the map by which he had set his route to the German-Swiss border.

Furthermore, Jones and Robinson remained blissfully unaware that they were once the guardians of two precious escape aids.

Our methods came in for a good deal of armchair criticism from certain Whitehall warriors, on the grounds that we were infringing the rules of combat, but I could find nothing condemning our actions in the Articles of the Geneva Convention, which I studied from A to Z. So we listened good-humouredly to pointed reflections on our moral code – and carried on.

As the months slipped by, our technique improved. We thought only in terms of faking and camouflage. We did our utmost to meet the demands of the prisoners themselves. When they wanted piano wire (which is extraordinarily strong and will support a great weight), we switched over to clothing parcels and inserted the thin wire inside the waistbands of grey flannel trousers. If a request came for a lens – to enable the escaper to read some of the microscopic details on his map – we devised a way of meeting it without any trouble. We sent one disguised as a stopper to an ordinary bottle of brilliantine. During a period when there was a widespread demand for compasses, we sent thousands of our magnetized blades quite openly.

With Operation Post-Box functioning smoothly, business was brisker than ever before, and the amount of escape equipment received by prisoners was fantastic. It was soon apparent that they were making good use of it. One return in 1942 showed that there were no fewer than 197 escapers in hiding in France, Belgium and Holland. Nearly a thousand were detained in neutral countries – the majority in Unoccupied France and in French North Africa, and nine at Gibraltar. A hundred and fifty prisoners had *attempted* to escape, but had unfortunately been recaptured. The same return indicated that out of over two hundred messages sent out to prisoners, almost a half had been received.

The number of attempted escapes was particularly pleasing, for it was three times as high as in the preceding month and brought the total of recorded attempts to more than eight hundred. It was logical to suppose that hundreds of other break-outs must have occurred in the same period, although news of them had not filtered through to our department. We obviously preferred successes to failures, but at the same time we knew that the more we could encourage men to try to get out, the greater would be the drag on enemy manpower in providing guards, escorts and search parties.

Apart from getting men back to fight again and harassing the enemy on the Home Front, we were also helping to establish valuable links with Resistance groups throughout the Occupied countries. The RAF outfits responsible for supplying these underground organizations with weapons, demolition stores, food, radio sets, clothing and information frequently applied to me for extra equipment and novel ideas. My Commanding Officer agreed to my co-operating, provided it did not interfere with my normal work. With characteristic bluntness, he pointed out that my reputation for 'crooked' methods was fast spreading. The next request for my services, he prophesied, would come from the Royal Navy. 'One day it will dawn on the First Sea Lord,' he observed drily, 'that although Britannia rules the waves, it's Clutty who waives the rules!'

One of my early RAF customers was a Wing Commander Farley, a first-class flier who told me a little about his night trips to the Continent. Security did not permit him to go into any great detail, but reading between the lines,

I guessed – wrongly, as it turned out – that he was concerned with transporting agents to and from France. He
himself did not mention the name of any particular
country, but the cigarette he offered me was a Gauloise,
so I drew my own conclusions. He was due to take some
passengers across that very night and had come along
hoping that I could equip him with a few useful escape
gadgets. After I had fixed him up with what he wanted,
he said he had another problem, which he would discuss
with me when he got back.

I regret to say that I never saw him again. His plane
was shot down over Germany and the luckless Farley
was killed. His job, however, continued, growing in scope
and importance, and the problem that had been bothering
Farley was eventually brought to me by one of his succes-
sors, Group Captain P. C. Pickard, better known by those
who saw the film *Target for To-night* as the captain of 'F'
for Freddie.

Rather more communicative than Wing Commander
Farley, Charles Pickard explained how the possibilities of
the night ferry service were being exploited to the full by
British Intelligence and how they were now using larger
aircraft to cope with the increasing two-way traffic. Airmen engaged on these clandestine trips were doubly
vulnerable, for before carrying out the actual mission,
they had to fly over the selected areas in broad daylight
to pick out likely landing zones.

According to Pickard, the main snag was that between
the reconnaissance and the real thing there could be a
change of wind that made landing difficult or out of the
question. What he sought was some gadget that would
indicate the direction of the wind during the hours of
darkness. He stressed that whatever device was used, it
would have to be one that could be easily handled by the

men and women belonging to the various Resistance groups.

It was some days later that I stumbled upon an obvious and inexpensive way of helping Pickard and his team of dare-devils. I was wandering round the plastic plant where the containers for our ration packs were made and happened to stroll into a room given over entirely to the manufacture of table-tennis balls. Lying on a work-bench were a number of balls which immediately attracted my attention, because they were still in a transparent state.

After examining one, I began to bounce it idly up and down, a vague idea stirring at the back of my mind. Suddenly the plastic ball split down the seam into two perfect hemispheres, both of which came to rest with the convex side uppermost. I gazed at the tiny mounds for so long that a workman, who had been eyeing me with a certain amount of suspicion, approached, picked up the pieces, and throwing them on to the bench, inquired if I wanted anything.

'Yes,' I said, pointing to the transparent balls, 'I'd like three of these – or rather, six halves. I shall also require, if you have them, a small tin of phosphorescent paint and a brush.'

Ten minutes later, the workman was evidently trying to puzzle out why I was carefully coating the insides of six half-balls with the paint he had brought me. Despite his curiosity, he asked no questions. I fancy he had decided it was best to humour me. If he could have seen me a couple of hours after that, he would have been convinced that I had taken leave of my senses, for the first thing I did on returning to Beaconsfield was to arrange the painted hemispheres on the window-sill of my office, exposing them to what was left of the light of day. My next move was to set them out on the lawn in a rough hexagon.

Then, waiting until it was quite dark, I made my way up to the roof of our country retreat and took up a position overlooking the lawn. Forty feet below, glowing and clearly visible, were my six fairy lights. Pickard's problem was solved.

Next day I was back at the plastics factory consulting with the experts. They quickly produced for me bigger and tougher half-balls in three sizes. I obtained a more powerful luminous paint, experimenting on the plastic bowls until I felt confident that they would be visible at night from a considerable height. I presented them to Pickard, told him how they could be used and asked him to let me know if they came up to expectations.

Three days elapsed before Pickard called to see me with his report. 'Absolutely wizard!' he enthused. 'I had your gadgets delivered by special plane with full instructions for the reception committees. You can take it from me that they worked like a charm. Next night one of my pilots flew over the landing zone at a thousand feet and could see it distinctly – a ruddy great arrow showing which way the wind was blowing. As the Resistance boys would say, '*Vous avez frappé le clou droit sur la tête*', Clutty! Or am I thinking of Terence Rattigan?'

Finding Pickard's fulsome praise rather embarrassing, I made several clumsy attempts to shoo him out, but it soon became apparent that my visitor was in no particular hurry to get away. Gradually it dawned on me that I had by no means finished with night operations over occupied territory. Either I was misreading the signs or Pickard was about to make a second call on our resources.

At last he decided to unburden himself. 'I don't like to bother you again, Clutty,' he began, 'but now that you've

improved our landing conditions, I was wondering if anything could be done about take-offs. The ideal contraption
would be some kind of easily portable searchlight that
the Resistance people could carry about without arous-
ing suspicion. What do you think?'

'I think you're a bloody nuisance,' I replied with feigned
severity. 'However, come back in a week's time and maybe I'll have something for you.'

A vague promise, indeed, but Pickard, who must have
been an incurable optimist, went away satisfied. As soon
as the door had closed behind him, I fished out of a drawer
the tattered exercise book in which I sometimes jotted
down germs of ideas, not only for escape devices but also
for commercial ventures that might prove useful after the
war. Skimming through the pages, I occasionally paused
to puzzle over such cryptic entries as: 'Margate Pier
Picture', 'Message Magnification', 'Name Tapes', 'Record
Sandwich', and so on. Then, I was suddenly pulled up
short by the three words, 'Torch Upright Flashing', and I
knew I was on the right track.

I have already referred to the special torch we manufactured to help airmen who were forced to bale out over
the sea. Extra long and ingeniously weighted, the torch
was clipped to the man's flying suit in such a way that it
could be released immediately after he hit the water. A
ten-foot cord prevented it from floating too far away
from its owner. On immersion, the torch switched itself
on and was so constructed that it continued to flash the
distress signal – three short, three long, three short – until
the battery was exhausted. As the lens stood up six inches
clear of the water, the winking light was visible at a distance of ten miles. A product of Halex Limited, the
SOS torch had scored an instant success with the RAF and
had eventually won the approval of the Royal Navy.

Glancing down at the almost illegible scribble which
had been the first step in a long and complicated process,
I asked myself why a torch, or at any rate a concentration
of torches, should not be used to facilitate take-offs on
Pickard's night sorties. Surely half a dozen powerful
beams, intelligently directed, would serve to light up the
improvised runways. Yes, torches would do the trick all
right. The only difficulty would be to camouflage them
so that the men and women of the Resistance could
wander about the country with them and not attract the
unwelcome attentions of the Occupying Power.

On the following day I had occasion to visit Messrs.
Blunt's and within a few minutes of leaving our country
residence, the answer was staring me in the face. Leary,
always an erratic driver, was exploring a narrow lane,
which he assured me was a short cut, when on taking a
bend a little too casually, he almost knocked down a lone
cyclist coming from the opposite direction. I swung round
anxiously, expecting to see both the man and his wobbl-
ing machine disappear into a ditch. To my great relief,
however, the poor fellow managed to regain his balance.
Leary's scathing comment was, 'Bloody clot! I'd like
to crack him on the bonce with his own bicycle pump!'

I was about to point out forcibly that Leary had been
entirely to blame, when something clicked. A bicycle
pump . . . a long hollow tube . . . ideal for conversion into
a torch . . . would never be queried by the Germans . . .
was it feasible?

After completing my business at the Old Kent Road
factory, I called on an engineer friend of mine and told
him exactly what I had in mind. He pursed his lips,
frowned, swore it was impossible, but in less than three
weeks he presented me with the finished article. What
had once been an ordinary bicycle pump had been

transformed into a torch capable of throwing out a beam
three hundred yards long and fanning out to a width of
seventy yards. There was a removable cap at the end
where the rubber connection was normally attached.
Underneath this had been fitted a thick lens, behind which
was a powerful bulb. The whole thing was operated by
three narrow accumulators encased in the body of the
pump. A feature that particularly appealed to me was that
these could be charged from a dynamo on the bicycle.
The 'pump' could be clipped to the bicycle and safely
left there until it was needed to help in providing a flare
path.

Pickard, of course, was overjoyed to receive the bicycle
pump torches. He arranged for them to be distributed to
our friends across the Channel and reported that everything was going well. His night fliers could see what they
were doing when they took off; the members of the Resistance organizations, setting off to provide flare paths
for British planes, pedalled with impunity past German
sentries and police. Our invention was doubly successful.

Never satisfied with a new device until it was giving
maximum service, I was not long in discovering an
auxiliary use for the floating torch. Some of our agents in
the occupied countries were provided with cameras for
photographing documents or worthwhile targets or events
that might have propaganda value. The problem of keeping the films under cover until they could be despatched to
England had been bothering our people for a long time.
One day, then, soon after the torch had gone into production, I suggested that the battery should be modified,
so that two cells should do the work of the usual three.
The third cell could be replaced by a brass cylinder into
which the spool of film could be inserted. Our 'overseas

representatives' were no longer worried about hiding their rolls of film.

Pickard never pestered me again, but I *did* invent one other small item that proved a blessing to the men and women we were dropping so regularly in enemy-held territory. By a natural sequence, my interest turned from films to cameras, especially as photography was a hobby I had pursued since boyhood. Now, I knew all about the miniature cameras that were on the market and was fully aware that they were being used to advantage by our cross-Channel agents. The task I set myself was to discover a reliable hiding-place for the smallest of these 'baby' models. Whatever I contrived had to fulfil two conditions. It had to escape notice if the owner was picked up without warning and submitted to a search. It had also to function as a camera without looking like one.

Hours of patient experiment led me eventually to the cigarette lighter. The experts at Messrs Blunt's fashioned a practical lighter, fractionally larger than the midget camera, that was a miracle of craftsmanship. It was even fitted with an extending view-finder, which enabled the photographer to focus on his subject whilst still holding the flame to his cigarette. To prove its efficiency, I took one with me to Beaconsfield, and without their knowing it, I snapped every officer on our establishment, if possible in characteristic poses. They were surprised, and in some cases acutely embarrassed, when I presented them with the prints. Another batch of promotions had recently come through and I had caught a couple of them squinting sideways at their brand-new crowns and pips. Crockatt, elevated to Brigadier, was looking particularly complacent.

I was sitting at my desk, chuckling over my candid camera shots, when the telephone suddenly shrilled.

Impatiently I snatched up the instrument and listened. It was a bad connection and a dozen odd accompanying noises emerged from the earpiece, but I immediately recognized the authoritative voice of a very dear friend of mine, Colonel Blacker.

'Is that you, Clutty?' he boomed above the cacophonous background.

Barely waiting for me to identify myself, and characteristically not bothering to tell me who he was, Blacker thundered on, 'Take your finger out and listen. I've invented a new gun, but the War House won't play. I need your help. My room, RAF Club, tomorrow morning.'

'I don't think I can – ' I began.

'Early,' cut in the Colonel, just as if I had never spoken. 'Better make it eight-thirty. Don't bother to knock. Knew you'd co-operate. Tell you all about it when I see you.'

'What sort of gun?' I managed to interpolate.

I heard an angry snort at the other end. 'It's certainly not a Flit-Gun!' And with that piece of negative information, the Colonel hung up on me. It was his way of reminding me that the enemy had ears.

Next morning, then, after an early breakfast, Leary drove me into town, dropping me outside my club in Piccadilly. I went straight to Blacker's room. I walked in without knocking, just as he had bade me. Propped up in bed by a mass of pillows, the Colonel, still in his pyjamas, was surrounded by a litter of drawings, plans and sheets of figures. He fixed me with his monocle, carelessly swept a sheaf of diagrams on to the floor, indicated that I was to sit down, and wasting no time on formalities, suddenly exploded, 'What we've got to do, Clutty, is to blast those bloody Germans right off the map!'

I murmured a polite agreement and waited for the Colonel to continue.

'Now, I've invented something really good. It's an anti-tank gun that's guaranteed to put the most heavily plated Tiger tank clean out of action. I started work on it pre-war, in my own workshop near Petworth. It's been a long and heart-breaking job, with no help from the people up top, but at last I'm all set to manufacture the prototype. All I need are a few controlled stores, and that, Clutty, is where you come in.'

'What about the War Office?' I began. 'Won't they – '

'Obstructionists of the worst sort,' was Blacker's succinct comment. 'Scared to handle anything new. Still living in the ballista and boiling-oil period. Some of those last-war dug-outs don't even know the Germans have *got* tanks.' He snorted contemptuously. 'No, Clutty, we'll have to by-pass officialdom, or by the time we produce the guns, the war will be over. I've heard a lot about your activities and I like your methods. That's why I've called you in.'

'I'll do what I can,' I said cautiously, 'but what exactly do you want?'

The Colonel shrugged. 'Nothing much for a man with your connections. A few steel tubes, a handful of fuses, a couple of dozen RAF twenty-five-pound bombs and a special piece of steel which I'll tell you about later. Oh yes, and a first-rate factory with men intelligent enough to put the gun together.' He picked up a blue-print and thrust it into my hands. 'It's as simple as that, but you can take it from me it'll punch a hole in a Royal Tiger.'

'But I know nothing about guns,' I objected.

'Doesn't matter a damn. Neither do half the brass hats in the War Office.'

'Who's going to foot the bill?'

'I'll attend to all that. You concentrate on the materials and the factory, and leave the rest to me. There's the list of essentials.' The Colonel passed me a sheet of paper and treated me to another of his hypnotic stares. 'Let me know when and where everything is assembled and I'll come along to direct operations. Any questions?'

I had a hundred questions, but cowed by that flashing eye, I left them unsaid. Evidently of the opinion that there was nothing further to discuss, the Colonel plunged back into his calculations. The audience was ended.

The morning was still young when I left the Club, so I seized the opportunity of doing a little personal shopping. At about eleven o'clock I took a bus to the Old Kent Road, intending to while away an hour in the gadget section, but as I was strolling towards the factory, my eye fell on a stack of scaffolding tubes, lying in the roadway near a building site. On a sudden impulse I searched round until I found the foreman. I showed him my special pass and then asked him point-blank if he would like to help the war effort. Although obviously taken aback by such a direct approach, he signified that he would do anything within reason.

I gestured towards the metal tubes. 'How much do you reckon those things are worth?'

'About forty quid.'

With bulging eyes he watched me fish out my wallet and extract a card bearing my private address. 'There you are, then,' I said, as I handed it to him. 'Get hold of a lorry, have the tubes delivered to that address right away, and I'll pay you fifty. Your driver can dump them near my garage.'

'I can't do that, guv'nor,' he protested. 'They'll sack me on the spot.'

'No, they won't,' I assured him. 'Tell your bosses

exactly what's happened and ask them to 'phone me. The number's on that card. It'll be perfectly all right. If you don't feel happy about it, come across to Blunt's with me and ring up *my* boss, Brigadier Crockatt. He'll confirm everything I've said.'

The foreman's gaze roved over the site and finally came to rest on an open lorry standing outside a partially erected building. He looked at the metal tubes and then at me. He nodded. The scaffolding, he informed me from the corner of his mouth, would be outside my garage within the hour.

Thanking God that the foreman had not called my bluff about ringing Crockatt, I hurried into the factory and lost no time in button-holing Dick Richards. I gave him a résumé of my conversation with Colonel Blacker and begged his assistance with the new gun. I would assemble all the parts, Blacker himself would supervise the work, and Messrs Blunt's would be well paid. All we really wanted was the use of certain machines and a little expert advice.

'But, Clutty, we've never handled an assignment of that nature,' said Dick dubiously. 'And with so many peculiar commitments – '

'One more won't hurt, Dick. Besides, this is bound to be a big thing, if it comes off. Blacker's by way of being a genius, you know. Speaks half a dozen languages fluently, has served in fourteen campaigns, and has an extraordinary knowledge of military history. He's an Ulsterman, and what he doesn't know about guns and other armaments isn't worth knowing. You'll enjoy working with him. Now, be a good chap and get me a line to the Air Ministry. I've got a pal there who can wangle one of the items.'

As soon as Dick put the call through for me, I knew he

was going to collaborate. He listened with a cynical grin to my end of a diplomatic conversation. When I put down the receiver, I was able to tell him that twenty-four aerial bombs had just been unofficially released and would be arriving at my flat on the morrow.

After that, everything went like clockwork. Woolwich provided the necessary fuses, and the Sheffield factory that was supplying steel for our compasses promised early delivery of the special piece of steel asked for by Blacker. Within a few days, the various components for the anti-tank gun were collected and transported to the factory. Blacker, armed with complicated diagrams and flashing monocle, made his appearance and right from the start his exuberance and enthusiasm infected the gun team. It was a new departure for the Old Kent Road technicians, but they threw themselves into the project with energy and determination. Without Messrs Blunt's as a base, the Colonel would never have produced his masterpiece.

Six months later, the first Blacker gun was tested. Satisfied that it would do all that its inventor had promised, we arranged for a demonstration before the Prime Minister at Chobham Ridge. Churchill was so impressed with the gun's accuracy and usefulness that he asked us to stage a repeat performance at Chequers for some of his colleagues. Everybody agreed that the device would revolutionize anti-tank warfare.

In spite of the Prime Minister's orders, the War Office obstructionists sat on the plans for weeks and it was only when Blacker caused several internal rockets to be fired that the plans were released, allowing the manufacturers to get on with their job.

What the obstructionists did *not* know was that Blacker, while designing this remarkable weapon (designated in Ordnance manuals as a Projector, Infantry,

Anti-Tank but familiarly known as the PIAT) had simultaneously designed a bigger and far more powerful model
known as the 'Bombard'. This too was put into immediate
production with devastating effect and both guns were
used in thousands. The PIAT was not an escape aid, of
course, but because it first saw the light of day in our
gadget factory, I have included its brief history in this
record. Its vital contribution towards the success of British
arms in the field is not likely to be disputed.

All in the Day's Work

The anti-tank gun was not the only offensive weapon we were called upon to manufacture. In sharp contrast to Colonel Blacker's tank killer was the dainty device we produced at the request of Colonel Bloch, a Free French officer who came to see me one morning, shortly after the PIAT incident, at my London office.

Tall and straight as a ramrod, his chest ablaze with campaign ribbons, my unexpected visitor addressed me in fluent English with only the faintest trace of foreign intonation.

'I have been given to understand' he said, without preamble, 'that you are a crook.'

'If you mean that I do not always observe the letter of the law,' I parried, 'then there's a certain amount of truth in what you've been told. I've been known to ignore "No Entry" signs when I've considered my journey really necessary.' I paused and then added with what I hoped was Gallic nonchalance, '*Je me sais débrouiller, monsieur.*'

My visitor smiled approvingly. 'A trait shared by most Frenchmen in Occupied France at the present time,' he remarked. 'They, too, know how to get out of difficulties. Under their German taskmasters, of course, they have to watch their opportunities. But I can assure you that most of them are, in their own way, still fighting the Boches. Morale remains high and they continue to harass the enemy whenever they can. They could probably do more – ' He paused and eyed me significantly ' – if they could rely on increased help from outside.'

I asked him what precisely he was getting at.

'Psychological warfare,' was his astonishing reply. 'My countrymen need some apparently harmless weapon which, whilst not lethal, will distract and irritate the Occupying Power. Many of them are already hitting back in a number of ways, especially through the medium of our underground organizations, but I was thinking rather in terms of the ordinary citizen in the street and wondering if he might be armed with an offensive device, innocent in appearance, that he could carry around in comparative safety. Have I made myself clear, monsieur?'

'As crystal,' I assured him. 'And if you'll give me time to go into the problem, I'll probably be able to produce something. I know exactly what you want – a minor irritant in everyday guise. Something small, too, that can be flown in and dropped in quantity. Look in next Monday in at about the same time.'

The officer thanked me and departed, leaving me to ponder on his strange request. Inspiration remained obstinately aloof, however, until later in the day when I was wandering round the compass factory, discussing the Frenchman's visit with Dick Richards. Passing the work bench where compasses were being made, I happened to glance at a stack of flat red tins containing gramophone needles. I remarked half-jocularly, half-seriously, 'Why not convert gramophone needles into miniature darts that can be fired at the Germans in some way? They would certainly cause annoyance, if nothing else. Maybe the French could use blow-pipes . . .'

Dick chuckled, but passed no comment. Then we moved on to watch a bomb-sight being tested and the French threat to the Occupation troops' peace of mind was temporarily forgotten.

Some days later, Dick rang me up and asked me to join him for lunch in the factory's board room. We chatted

on a wide variety of subjects during the meal, but all the
time I had an impression that my host was concealing
something from me. He seemed preoccupied and once or
twice I surprised a ghost of a grin when he thought I was
not looking in his direction.

Soon after the coffee was brought in, Dick took from
his pocket what looked for all the world like a fountain-
pen. Bidding me pay attention, he unscrewed the cap and
then pointed the barrel towards the door of the board
room. There was a sharp 'ping' and a scarcely audible
thud as a tiny steel dart whizzed through the air and
embedded itself in the wood just above the door handle.
Fascinated, I went over to investigate.

It was a gramophone needle.

'So it works!' I cried excitedly. 'What's its range?'

Dick laughed. 'Forty feet – and uncannily accurate.
Have a good look at it.'

I did. Attached to the blunt end of the needle was a
little cluster of shaving-brush hairs daintily trimmed, and
the barrel had been rifled.

Dick then showed me the 'gun'. He explained that the
designer had copied the principle of the old-fashioned
airgun. The dart was propelled by two powerful springs
inside a delicately rifled barrel which fitted on the end of
the pen and was no bigger than a genuine pen nib. To
fire the weapon, all one had to do was to press down the
pen clip and then release it. I actually tried a couple of
shots. Dick was quite right. The finely rifled dart sped
unerringly to its target. A real precision job, and according to Dick, remarkably cheap to produce.

I had little doubt that this wicked toy would delight
the hearts of all loyal Frenchmen. I was naturally eager
to hand over the prototype to the rangy officer who had
approached me the week before, but on second thoughts

I decided to offer it to our own people first. Consequently I took the superficially ridiculous weapon along to the War Office and demonstrated its capabilities – admittedly very limited – to certain senior officers. I suggested that such a gadget could have a powerful psychological value. All we had to do was to start a rumour in Paris that the darts were poisoned. Then our French agents and supporters could take pot-shots at passing Germans from windows, from stationary vehicles, even from boulevard cafés, secure in the knowledge that their victims would not linger to cross-examine bystanders, but would undoubtedly make for the nearest hospital. Alarm and despondency could be spread on an incalculable scale.

I shall never forget the frigid atmosphere conjured up by my innocent proposals.

'Good God, man!' growled a Major-General. 'Do you want us to be impeached at Geneva for using poison?'

'Not at all, sir,' I replied. 'The joke would be on the Germans when they discovered that the darts were *not* poisoned.'

It was evident from the shocked expressions around me that my audience did not share my peculiar sense of humour. 'Take the damned thing away!' was the Major-General's irate verdict.

So two days later I reluctantly handed over the needle-gun to Colonel Bloch. His enthusiastic reception of our latest gadget and his gloating forecast of the uses to which it would be put by our cross-Channel neighbours led me to suspect that he was unlikely to be troubled by thoughts of the Geneva Convention. He took the 'gun' away and I never saw him again. It was not, in fact, until several months had elapsed that I was informed by a friend, who had been in France on special service, that the crazy Parisians were actually firing steel darts into the cheeks

and necks of the Occupation troops and creating wholesale panic by spreading a cock-and-bull yarn to the effect
that the missiles were poisoned.

'The Jerries are in a blue funk,' my friend told me gleefully. 'Trust the French to think up such a crafty method
of harrying the Hun.'

I smiled appreciatively, but said nothing. . . .

Like the PIAT, the needle-gun was not an escape aid, but
my next effort was certainly intended to fall within that
category. That I was forced to abandon the project owing
to circumstances beyond my control is a regrettable fact.
That the story of my first large-scale bloomer makes
amusing reading is sufficient warrant for its inclusion in
this very personal document.

It all began one evening at an RAF station where I had
been lecturing on the technique of escape and the duties
of a prisoner-of-war. Over a friendly drink in the officers'
mess afterwards, I was buttonholed by a lugubrious pilot,
who complained dismally of the intense cold in the cock-
pit of a plane, especially on night operations. If only a
bowl of hot soup could be made available, the air crews
would accept with philosophic detachment the irregular
hours and low temperatures of nocturnal sorties. A
thermos flask of black coffee was stimulating, but something more nourishing was desirable. Ration packs and
comic pens and silk maps were all very well, he grumbled,
but what about something warm and filling for the Ham-
burg run, for instance?

Now, before the war, when I was connected with the
food business, I had conducted experiments with self-
heating cans of soup, but had never pursued the idea com-
mercially. My conversation with the disgruntled flying
officer encouraged me to dig out a note-book compiled

during my earlier labours and to put my previous theories to the test.

Basically the process was childishly simple. A small can of soup was fixed inside a larger tin containing quicklime. Part of the space between the two tins served as a separate compartment for water. The top and bottom of the outer can were clearly indicated. To heat the soup, all one had to do was to turn the whole contraption upside-down after punching a couple of holes through which the water could trickle on to the quicklime. The heat thus generated was sufficient to bring the soup to boiling point in forty seconds.

After several successful attempts with different brands of soup, I decided it was time to introduce my device to the RAF Quartermaster's department. Accordingly I sent off a number of samples. They were not even acknowledged by those to whom they were addressed.

Indignant at such cavalier treatment, I made up my mind to force the issue. I was determined that at least my can of self-heating soup should be seen and given a trial. I resolved to despatch it in a form that could not easily be overlooked.

I had a large wooden crate made. In the centre of this giant box – it was a six-foot cube – I suspended a solitary can of soup, artistically labelled 'DANGER'. I then marked the outsize packing-case 'PERSONAL' and forwarded it to the head of the purchasing organization at Adastral House, Kingsway. I had little doubt that the arrival of such a monstrous container would arouse curiosity if nothing else. Taking up a strategic position near the telephone, I now sat back and waited developments.

When the expected call came through, I cheerfully admitted that I had sent the crate . . . Yes, the labelling on the tin was perfectly justified . . . With my tongue

in my cheek I denied any intention on my part of being
disrespectful . . . I *did* consider the matter urgent . . . No,
I had no objection to popping round and explaining what
it was all about . . . It would be a pleasure . . .

I hurried across to the Ministry and was immediately
ushered into the presence of a grim-faced Air Commodore,
who wasted no time on preliminaries. Pointing to my tin
of soup, which was standing in the very centre of his
beautifully polished desk, he demanded abruptly what
the devil it was. He listened sceptically to my glowing
account of the self-heating can. He seemed totally un-
impressed by my references to its efficiency and cheap-
ness. Nevertheless, when I had finished my glib sales-talk,
he asked me to demonstrate the effectiveness of what he
was pleased to term my invention.

With a flourish I whisked a bradawl from my pocket,
handed it over and bade the Air Commodore punch the
holes in the tin with his own hands. I wanted him, I art-
fully insinuated, to have personal experience of the un-
complicated nature of my gadget. Simplicity of operation
was its most attractive feature. An airman, busy· at
the controls, could start the heating process single-
handed.

Sheepishly he poked a couple of holes in the tin, in
obedience to my instructions. We then waited – but not
for long.

What went wrong I cannot imagine. With a celerity I
should never have dreamed possible, the tin suddenly
began to give off a fiercely concentrated heat. A gentle
hissing sound from within swelled to an ominous fizzing
and gurgling. Then, with a reverberating boom, the canis-
ter exploded, ejecting its scalding contents all over the
furniture and starting fires in every direction.

From the outer office in rushed panic-stricken clerks

wielding stirrup pumps and extinguishers. Streams of water and spurting jets of carbon tetrachloride were played on the dancing flames. The carpeted floor was awash; smoke still spiralled ceilingwards; a charred black patch disfigured the surface of the desk. The stench was nauseating – a pungent combination of smouldering paint-work, carbide, singed carpets and burnt vegetable matter. And standing in the middle of his ravaged room was the man whose baleful glare informed me unequivocally that he was unlikely to evince any further interest in my self-heating soup.

Nervously clutching my hat, I edged strategically doorwards.

Service communications in wartime – particularly with our agents – are naturally a most closely guarded secret. They were the one thing that I steered clear of, and nothing would make me discuss anything to do with these operations outside our own organization.

Apart from being far too complicated for my rather slow brain, and too difficult to absorb, I was scared to death that any of my own staff might accidentally communicate to some unauthorized person something they had seen or heard. That would have sent the balloon up for the whole of my section, so anything in this line that came my way I passed on as quickly as I could to others to test and pronounce upon.

I had some disappointments, however, in my attempts to contribute to this tricky sector of the war effort. Here is an example.

One morning about 7.30 my office door opened and a young man walked in. (On days when I was working at the War Office I usually turned up before breakfast.) He was a cripple, and from his appearance and his very

shabby suit it was obvious that he was not very well off.
He told me he was 27 years old, and a bad attack of polio
a year or two previously had prevented him from getting
any job at which he could be useful. For the past six
months he had been unsuccessfully offering his talents to
the Services, but no one was willing to let him put on a
uniform.

'Well,' I asked him, 'what can you do?'

'I can draw on a very small scale,' he answered.

'How small?'

'Like this,' and he produced a tiny box lined with cotton
wool. From it he took a grain of rice, on one side of which
I could just see a drawing; when I looked at it through a
magnifying glass I saw that it was a picture of West-
minster Abbey!

'Do you draw like this under a magnifying glass?' I
asked him.

'No, I draw with the naked eye – and it makes me very
tired.'

This intrigued me, so I helped him downstairs and took
him out for breakfast. I suspected from the way he
tackled his food that he was not getting enough to eat. I
learned that he lived in a small riverside village with his
sixty-year-old widowed mother and his three brothers and
sisters; she herself had to go out to work in a factory to
support them all. While we were having breakfast, Laker
(which is not his real name) took from his pocket another
tiny box, in which were more specimens of his work. One
was a postage stamp with the Lord's Prayer written out in
full on the back; another was an ordinary match with a
wedge-shaped piece cut from the middle third of the
match so that it could slide freely in and out; underneath this, on the wood of the match, a message was
written.

I realized that I had stumbled upon a wizard, but alas, things did not work out as I had hoped.

'Could you reduce a map by your method?' I asked him.

'I am sure I could,' he replied.

Later, back in my office, I showed him some of my early silk and thin paper maps, which surprised him by their clarity, for they showed over 70,000 names in an area 20 inches square.

'There you are,' I told him. 'If you can reduce, say, a quarter of this to about 2 inches square in a month, to show what you can do, I will give you £10. Here is £5 on account.'

Laker seemed very grateful and promised to let me have the sample in a month's time. I wished him luck and he went away feeling that at last he could really be of some use. I knew it was useless to waste any time trying to persuade the Service departments to offer him a job in uniform, but since I had obviously hit upon a most unusual man who could perform useful service to our cause, I approached the Treasury to see whether there was some loophole through which he could be smuggled in. But they produced one objection after another. Suppose he 'died on us' – they might have to pay out a pension. In any case the appointment would be creating a precedent, and there was no knowing where that might lead to. So, rather than batter my head against a brick wall, I decided to pay him a small weekly wage out of my own pocket.

After no more than a fortnight Laker came to my office again and to my astonishment laid before me a small piece of thin paper exactly two inches square, upon which, in six colours, he had reduced exactly one quarter of the map I had given him – and drawn it with the naked eye. Feeling very excited, I helped Laker to my car and drove him off to one of the hush-hush map departments in the country to show off my prodigy.

When he had recovered from his surprise, the head mapper studied Laker's effort and it was not long before his face dropped with disappointment.

'Brilliant work,' he told us, 'but unfortunately this remarkable reduction is *not to scale.*'

When we left the mappers, as I didn't wish to depress the fellow I gave him other experiments to do—which seemed to buoy him up with encouragement.

Two days later I received a letter from his mother to say that her son had died after a stroke. That fellow died from a broken heart, feeling he was just not wanted.

I mention this case as an example of the eager way in which outsiders from every source daily tried to contribute their efforts to the gigantic cause we had to pursue.

An experiment of more humorous character – though strictly speaking not my pigeon – worked out well in practice, or so I was told. Before the war I was actively associated with a large food manufacturing firm, whose managing director, a relative of mine, was always game for a good stunt. He was just as enthusiastic about propaganda as I was, and never charged a penny for his services. I got this man's firm to make small cubes of concentrated food; into a small proportion of these cubes I had inserted little pieces of paper on which was printed information about the numbers of Germans killed in RAF raids. These concentrated foods then made their appearance in cargoes of foodstuffs bought, stolen or otherwise imported from the Scandinavian countries. Many German housewives must have been horrified to find some telling enemy propaganda floating in their saucepans of soup.

One morning I received a letter, which came to me via
Switzerland, and there was one item that prompted me
to put through an urgent call to the Air Ministry. I had
thought of a way in which my methods could be used to
some advantage.

There was only a slight delay before I was through to
the Air Ministry exchange.

'Clayton Hutton speaking,' I said. 'Put me on to
"Bomber" Harris.'

'Air Marshal Sir Arthur Harris is engaged,' a female
voice frigidly informed me. 'Will anybody else do?'

'Not unless you can get me Hermann Goering!'

I listened to the operator's horrified gasp, replaced the
receiver and sent for a driver.

Leary drove me to Bomber Command and in less than
ten minutes I had managed to talk my way into the presence of Air Marshal Sir Arthur Harris. I fancy he would
have hurled me back into the corridor with his own hands,
had I not quickly reminded him that I had supplied his
bomber crews with escape boots. Visibly controlling his
irritation, he said he could spare me five minutes.

I startled him by striding over to a tremendous wall map
of Berlin. 'This,' I said, stabbing confidently with my forefinger, 'is a huge church in the Lindenstrasse, which runs
in this direction. Just about here' – I gave the map another
authoritative prod – 'is Number Thirty-Two. Now, sir, I
know what a wonderful precision job Wing-Commander
Guy Gibson and his boys did when they destroyed the
Möhne and Eder dams. What I want to know is – could
your chaps actually blast a particular building – this one,
for instance?'

'Why that one?' barked Harris.

'I'll tell you why, sir. This letter arrived by the morning post.' I took the letter from my pocket and unfolded

it whilst I was speaking. 'It's from a pre-war friend of mine who was living in Berlin when I was there filming about sixteen years ago. I don't know where he is now, because there's no address on the letter. All I can say for certain is that it was posted in Switzerland. But this is the significant paragraph. With your permission, sir, I'll read it to you. My pal's writing isn't very legible.'

Harris uttered what I took to be an affirmative grunt, so I carried on.

'He refers to some work we did together, and then he says this : "You'll be surprised to hear what has happened to your old studio in the Lindenstrasse, Number Thirty-Two, not far from the big church, remember? Well, believe it or not, but it's now being used by Doctor Goebbels for all his film propaganda. He practically lives there. I understand he's specializing at the moment on documentary films, shot from German submarines immediately after successful engagements, showing the actual sinking of torpedoed British ships. I suppose he distributes the stuff all over Germany and the Occupied countries to prove that the *Oberkommando der Kriegsmarine* is winning the war at sea. Funny to think that the building where we used to meet so often is now one of the Propaganda Minister's show-places." And the rest of the letter concerns personal matters, so I won't bore you with it. The point is – it would be a fine smack in the eye for Gabby Goebbels if your lads called with their visiting-cards.'

'Is that letter dated?' was 'Bomber' Harris's next question.

'Unfortunately, no.'

'So it might have been written months ago and in the meantime Goebbels could have moved his film unit to some other part of Berlin.'

'That's true, sir,' I agreed. 'That's why I propose to have all the data checked. I needn't tell you that our organization exists to encourage and facilitate escapes from POW camps. Now we have – or think we have – a fool-proof method of communicating with the men in the camps. My plan is to instruct an escaper to make for Berlin after he breaks out and investigate this Lindenstrasse set-up. If all goes well, and if the escaper informs us that Goebbels is still operating from Number Thirty-Two, Lindenstrasse, will you arrange a spot of demolition?'

'Bomber' Harris reflected for a few moments and then shook his head regretfully. 'It's an attractive scheme, but in my opinion it would be suicidal to send an escaped prisoner into Berlin on what might, after all, turn out to be a wild-goose chase. I'm sorry, but I'm not going to commit myself at this stage. All I'm prepared to say right now is that if circumstances warrant a bombing raid in that particular area of the German capital, I'll organize one. The information you have given me may very well influence any future decision I shall make. That's the best I can do for you.'

The bomber chief shuffled the papers on his desk and glanced down rather pointedly at his wrist watch, so taking the hint, I tactfully withdrew. The interview had not been altogether unsatisfactory. I had not managed to extract a firm promise that Number 32, Lindenstrasse, would be bombed, but at least I had created an interest in the right quarters.

Several months later I had occasion to call on 'Bomber' Harris again. He blandly informed me that his boys had carried out a saturation raid on a certain district of Berlin during the previous night. My former studio, he added with a twinkle in his eye, had been obliterated. . . .

Back at Beaconsfield I was kept as busy as ever, first of all by a chance discovery within reasonable walking distance of our headquarters, secondly by an exciting battle with the bureaucrats in connection with a new escape aid I had conceived, and thirdly by an invention that almost landed me in trouble with MI 5.

My lucky find, believe it or not, was a disused grave-yard, which I came across one morning towards the end of a gentle stroll in the lovely country surrounding our mansion. I was plodding across a field, when I suddenly spotted several headstones – grey, weather-beaten, their inscriptions nearly indecipherable. As I drew near, I noticed many more, of varying heights and shapes, scattered over a fairly wide area. They occupied about two acres of ground, a roughly rectangular patch, with three sides merging into the adjoining farm land and the fourth bounded by a long straggling hedge. A beady-eyed old man was trimming this hedge and viewing my approach with thinly veiled suspicion.

The ancient waited until I was only three or four yards away, lowered his shears and fluted some inarticulate form of greeting.

'Good-day to you, sir,' I bade him politely. 'I'd no idea there was a cemetery up here. When was it last used?'

'Nigh on seventy years ago,' was the quavering reply.

Thinking vaguely of Harris in *Three Men in a Boat*, I invited the old countryman to show me round. He seemed curiously reluctant to move and continued to point the shears in my direction until I offered him half a crown. A vulturine claw grabbed the coin, the cutters were placed on top of a stone slab, and away we went on a leisurely tour of the tombs, my superannuated guide pausing every few yards to point out the final resting-place of some local village worthy.

I was not listening, for I was concentrating on the great empty stretches of meadow and arable land lying beyond the three vanished boundaries of this outlandish cemetery. No farms, no houses, not even a shed, and apart from my venerable companion, not a living soul in sight. If I was not mistaken, this desolate region was precisely what I had been looking for. Isolated, well off the beaten track, and yet not too far away from our HQ. It seemed ideal for the purpose I had in mind.

We had now reached a dip in the corner of the cemetery. In the next field, about a dozen yards distant, stood a huge oak-tree, its prolific branches offering the natural cover I was seeking. I knew that further search was unnecessary. The ground under the oak would meet my requirements.

A second half-crown purchased the name and address of the farmer who owned the land, with instructions for getting there thrown in as a grudging extra. I set off at once, in the general direction of a wooded knoll, round which I circled until I stumbled upon a deeply rutted cart-track. I followed this for at least half a mile, and at last, exactly as the old hedger had said, it petered out in the farmyard itself. When I pushed open the creaking gate, a chain rattled, a dog barked, hens squawked, and a friendly-looking fellow in corduroy breeches and a check shirt emerged from a nearby barn.

I introduced myself, told him I was engaged on highly important work of a confidential nature, described the piece of ground that had caught my eye and inquired if I could rent it from him. He readily agreed to let me have the land, and because it was for the war effort, waved aside any suggestion of payment. When I asked if he had any objection to my putting up a small building on the site, he replied, 'You can stick a bloody cinema there for all I care, so long as you take it away when the war's over!'

Delighted with my morning's work, I returned to our headquarters, took a car from the vehicle pool and drove out to a village fifteen miles outside Beaconsfield. There I enlisted the services of a casual labourer – an ageing rustic of limited intelligence and incredible muscular development. I ran him out to the disused cemetery, showed him the oak-tree and explained in simple terms that I wanted him to construct an underground room beneath its spreading branches.

Clearly of the opinion that he was dealing with a lunatic, my startled assistant edged away nervously. 'A room, sir?' he demanded, his bushy eyebrows lifting interrogatively. 'Under yon tree?'

'That's right. About twenty by twelve by eight, the finished job to look like a burial vault, with its entrance facing the tombstones. Keep the roof as near ground level as possible and it might be a good idea to camouflage it with turfs.'

There was a long pause while the poor fellow endeavoured to digest my instructions. He appeared to be muttering to himself. Finally, he clung desperately to what were probably the only two words he had understood. 'With turfs, sir,' he said. 'I see.'

'I'll provide all the materials and have them dumped here. I imagine you've got your own tools, but if there's anything special you want, just let me know. Now, you'll need timber for shoring, plenty of bricks, mortar and a few of those things.' I indicated the flat burial slabs in the graveyard and added tentatively, 'I don't suppose we could borrow two or three of those.'

His expression of incredulous horror suggested that my village labourer was not in favour of employing the material that was ready to hand. He was strongly opposed to 'larkin' about with a man's last 'ome', as he put it. His disapproving attitude gave me the impression that he saw me as a sinister figure, dodging in and out of the tombstones at dead of night, opening coffins and carrying their grisly contents back to my subterranean lair for a necrophagous orgy. I had to exert all my powers of persuasion to convince him that I was acting on behalf of an army organization, and even then he flatly refused to co-operate until I gave him my most solemn assurance that I would buy all the stone-work from one of the Beaconsfield undertakers.

For two or three weeks I was busy arranging with the Transport Officers of neighbouring units for stray three-tonners to pick up illicit loads of building material. For security reasons, the drivers were ordered to deliver at the farm and from there the various items were transferred to the site in a hand-cart. The farmer, entering into the spirit of the thing, loaned me one of his men, and shortly after the actual building programme started, the ancient who had first conducted me round the cemetery insisted on joining our team. With four of us attacking with picks and shovels, the immense hole soon began to take shape.

But forsaking the excavations for a moment, I must now explain the circumstances that had constrained me to seek a hide-out at that particular time.

At the beginning of my career as a gadget expert, when I had only a handful of escape devices to my credit, most of my brother officers had chosen to regard my activities

with unqualified contempt. They classified me as a mad-
man, ridiculing many of my inventions, sniggering at my
un-military behaviour, and visiting my department only
when they had to. Then gradually, as my 'toys' grew in
number and were eagerly sought after by combatant
officers and men of the rapidly expanding RAF, the same
people who had treated me so abominably began to drop
in my office at all hours, ostensibly to admire my latest
contraption, but covertly to pocket any attractive articles
that took their fancy. Some of the favourite collectors'
items were the escape pen, silk maps. 'baby' compasses,
SOS torches, and if the scroungers were particularly
shameless, pilots' escape boots.

Naturally, I was not worried about the monetary value
of the various odds and ends that disappeared in this
manner. What *did* concern me was the fact that security
regulations were being flagrantly ignored and that these
wholesale depredations made a mockery of my own
attempts to keep our business hush-hush. I saw little point
in warning my staff about the danger of careless talk,
when dozens of outsiders were treating my office as a sort
of help-yourself, don't-pay gadget shop. I felt sure that
some of these souvenir hunters were quite capable of
trying to impress friends and relatives by showing them
my top secret equipment; others would not be beyond
losing some of it. Apart from anything else, this easy-
going attitude infuriated me.

Long before I had happened upon the burial ground,
therefore, I had been searching for a suitable cache in
which to house my more valuable material, together with
reserve stocks of all fast-moving goods. The difficulty had
been to find a place accessible to me but inaccessible to
the rest of our headquarters staff. An underground vault
on the edge of a cemetery that had not been used for

seventy years would at least tend to discourage casual callers.

At last my hide-out was ready for occupation. Cleverly camouflaged, with a flight of stone steps on the cemetery side as its only entrance, it blended perfectly with its surroundings. It was spacious and surprisingly well ventilated. There were only two snags. Lighting and heating had to be by oil. In spite of these drawbacks, my den was very dry, and when my oil heater was working, sufficiently warm even in the coldest weather.

Little by little I carried out the transfer of floor covering, furniture, shelves and hundreds of escape devices to this unorthodox store-room. I went there only at night, whether I was depositing gadgets or taking them away, and always on my own. Frequently, when my day's work was done, I would sneak away quietly to the vault to experiment with some new contrivance, and there I would sit at my desk, alone among the dead, well into the small hours. Nobody, as I then thought, was aware of my underground activities, and so I continued to operate beneath my oak, snug and undisturbed, right through to the end of the war.

That I was not quite as crafty as I had imagined emerged in 1952 during a lecture tour in America. After I had told a delightfully enthusiastic St Louis audience about my personal contribution to the escape scheme, a dinner was held in my honour. One of the guests happened to be an American officer who had been attached to our Beaconsfield headquarters for liaison purposes. As he had spent a lot of time in my department, he had been asked to propose a toast to the visiting lecturer. I listened complacently to his witty references to my 'crooked' methods, but I was shaken to the core when he concluded his remarks with a detailed description of my burrow and the devious route I used to follow on my nocturnal sorties.

I approached him later in the evening and inquired how he had managed to unearth my secret.

'I was coming back from a late date one night and I saw you sneaking out, Major, so being naturally curious, I decided to tail you. When you led me to that bone-yard, you sure scared the hell out of me. Guess I had you tabbed Krafft-Ebing-wise until I took a peek into that vault.'

'Why follow me at all?' I asked him. 'I might have been going out for an evening stroll.'

The American officer raised a quizzical eyebrow. 'Not at twenty minutes after midnight, Major,' he drawled. 'And I forgot to mention you were toting a couple of out-size grips. I didn't have to be Philo Vance to guess you weren't out there for health reasons!'

'Tell me,' I said, 'what was I doing the night you played Private Eye?'

'I guess you were fooling around with a gramophone record.'

My American friend was right. I *had* been exploring the possibilities of an ordinary record, with a view to using it as a hiding-place, for it was during my first week in the bunker that I had been confronted with a new problem. For some time we had been sending maps and paper money into the camps concealed under the end-papers of books and we had just been informed that the enemy had tumbled to our little game. According to our informant, searchers were automatically ripping the covers off all books arriving in welfare parcels. We had therefore been advised to employ an alternative form of carrier.

I remember how I took to pieces and reassembled all manner of recreational gear, until one night I hit upon the idea of secreting maps and money in gramophone records. My unseen watcher must have seen me at the very moment I was studying one.

A thorough examination had convinced me that special dies could be manufactured to produce records containing a shallow rectangular cavity between the two sides, underneath the label. So, eager to try out my theory, I had Leary drive me to the record-making plant of a well-known gramophone company, only to find most of the forty-ton presses idle and shrouded in dust covers. The man I talked to was not very hopeful and said that he doubted very much whether his managing director would open the presses at all, let alone agree to the modifications I had suggested. Much as he would have enjoyed helping me, he dared not take action off his own bat. My best plan was to tackle the managing director personally. With official support, he assured me, he would do anything I wished.

No more than five feet high, and like most little men, puffed up with his own conceit and self-importance, the managing director received me frigidly, listened to my request and then practically ordered me out of his office. Although I longed to put my foot behind him. I quietly reminded him that he would be helping us to win the war if he gave his consent and begged him to change his mind. My second appeal drew from him a childish exhibition of temper and a storm of vicious abuse. His angry tirade ended with these significant words: 'What the devil do you think our sister companies in Germany will say after the war?'

It was clearly a waste of time to argue with him. I walked straight out of his office, down to where Leary was waiting, and bade him drive me to the War Office, where things moved fast. An official complaint in the right quarters, a telephone conversation at a fairly high level,

The R.A.F. ration pack, Mark IV, contained a map, 12 Horlicks tablets, a tube of cream, a packet of water-purifying tablets, a bar of chocolate, adhesive tape, compass, 12 benzedrine tablets, matches, needle and thread. Emptied of its contents, it served as a water-bottle.

The stopper held not only a compass but, behind that, a watch.

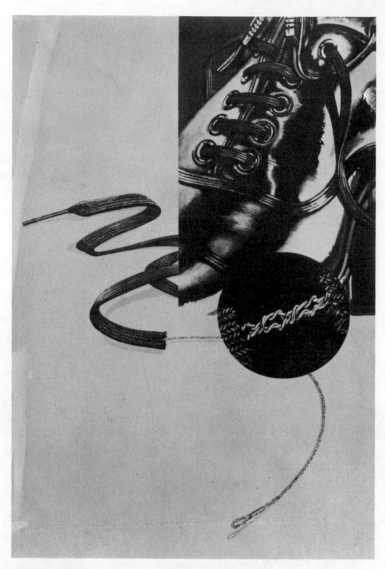

In flying-boot laces, the tags of which were magnetized, was often included a flexible "Gigli" saw, which could cut through a steel bar.

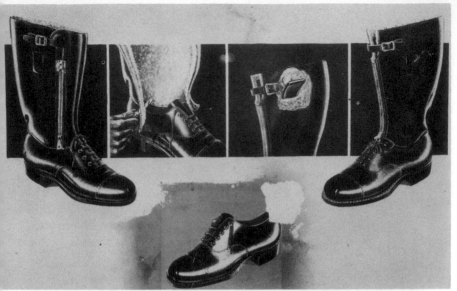

(*Above*) The flying boot that had everything. With a small knife, concealed in the cloth loop, the upper portion could be cut away, leaving the one item every escaper wanted—civilian shoes. The upper portion could be used to make a warm, fur-lined waistcoat. (*Below*) Accessible through a hinged flap in the straight edge of the heel, a cavity (*shown dissected*) held silk maps, a compass and a small file. Between two layers of the rubber or composition (held together by small screws) was a further hiding-place for documents, etc.

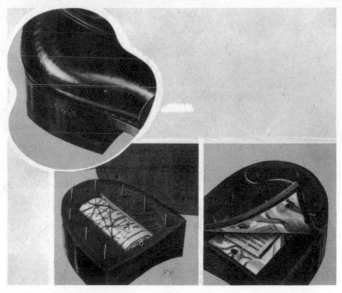

(*Left*) Old, well-chewed pencil stubs, collected from many schoolrooms, were easily converted to compasses. (*Below*) In an intricately constructed chess set, the base of the king might contain a crystal wireless set and the walls of the box, maps.

Even an ordinary playing card could conceal a map behind a false back. A whole pack covered exactly one country, and the joker contained the key.

A captured shove-ha'penny board which the Germans found "hard to understand" but which "seemed to amuse the British prisoners for hours on end." Concealed in the underside were chessmen, packs of cards, counters, pencils, etc. Many of these items were far from innocent, and the more obviously "secret" objects were hidden beneath the strengthening center-board.

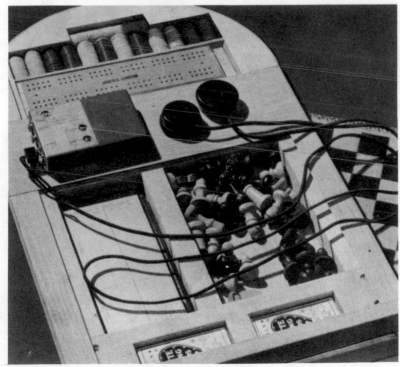

(*Above*) Within the skeleton of this wooden games box were maps, compasses, saws, etc. Between the walls were plastic photographic maps, compressed, of various sites in enemy territory. When pressure was released they rose in relief to scale. (*Below*) In some cases a colored plastic scale model might be concealed in the top or bottom of a games box. In the early days of plastic manufacture there was some difficulty in finding a soft plastic which not only could be compressed but which would rise easily to its proper scale height when released. By shining a light on the model, the lengths of shadows cast could be envisaged in case a prisoner wished to avail himself of such shadows in attempting an escape.

Reversible uniforms were a specialty. Officers and O.R.s were entitled to receive new uniforms in the camps. This picture of a "trick" uniform shows how, when the lining was removed, a "civvy" suit was revealed.

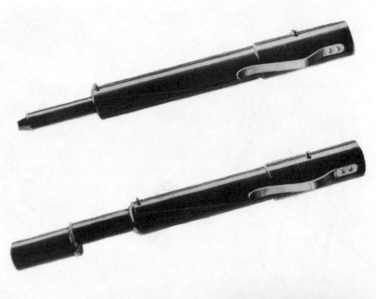

This pocket-gun's powerful spring fired a gramophone-needle dart (*inset*).

and within twenty minutes I was on my way back to the factory, but sitting alongside me in the car was a gentleman in whose pocket was a warrant for the arrest of the managing director.

What had happened during my absence to bring about a change of heart, I shall never know. Perhaps the fellow had rung up our headquarters and checked my *bona fides*. Or he might have felt ashamed of his earlier cantankerousness, although that was most unlikely. Whatever the cause, however, his manner had undergone a radical alteration. He welcomed us with great civility, apologized for his former irritability, and without any further prompting from me, offered to put a number of presses at my disposal. He even suggested that I should seek the advice of his technical experts. I graciously allowed him to persuade me to begin my experiments on the following day, shook hands to seal the bargain and withdrew in triumph. The presence of my companion, who had merely hovered in the background with an enigmatic expression on his face, had no doubt had its effect. Although he had played no part in it, he said he had enjoyed the little scene, and later, when I dropped him in Whitehall, he insisted on presenting me with the unused warrant.

And so we went into the gramophone record business in a big way, for it was soon proved that the hiding-place I had envisaged was a practical proposition. In order not to offend the German taste in music, we carefully avoided reproducing the works of any Jewish composers, concentrating mainly on Wagner and Beethoven, and cheerfully accepting the fact that our gifts were more likely to entertain the German guards than the British prisoners. The real irony was that the latter derived most benefit from our excellent records by breaking them, a circumstance that led me to christen the whole affair 'Operation Smash-Hit'.

We packed our discs in light wooden cases, wrapped in brown paper and labelled 'Gramophone Pressing Co. Ltd.' There was almost as much escaping material in the packing as there was in the actual records.

The gramophone records served us well as carriers, but eventually the Germans tumbled to our trickery. Once the scheme was blown and we knew that the discs were being smashed on arrival at the camps by the enemy parcel censors, we abandoned that particular method of sending out maps and foreign currency. The many friends we had made at the record plant were genuinely sorry to see us go. The managing director *said* he regretted our departure, but the smirk on his face indicated that he was glad to see the back of us.

The sequel to Operation Smash-Hit occurred two years after Germany was beaten. I was sitting in the lounge bar of a country hotel, enjoying a glass of Dubonnet before lunch, when who should come strutting fussily in but the undersized managing director and a prosperous-looking business man, whose square head and short bull neck proclaimed him to be a German. The precious pair were probably forging a new trade link to replace the one shattered by the outbreak of war in 1939. The record king deliberately ignored me, but on my way out I made a point of crossing over to him, and without saying a word, pushed the warrant for his arrest under his nose. When he realized how near he had been to serving a prison sentence, he almost collapsed. As I left the bar, I heard him calling feebly for a large brandy. I hope it choked him. . . .

The invention that involved me with MI 5 was not one of mine, although I *did* make arrangements for its manufacture on behalf of the RAF. Nor was it an escape device. Like the PIAT gun, however, it deserves a place in this record in so far as its checkered history sheds considerable light on the mysterious workings of the bureaucratic mind. I refer to an article that now sells by the million all over the world – the ball-point pen.

I was first introduced to this remarkable gadget in the office of a friend of mine at the Air Ministry. After explaining to me that at certain altitudes the ordinary fountain-pen was adversely affected by atmospheric pressure and that in some cases the rubber sac holding the ink had been known to burst, he handed me a pen which, he assured me, operated on an entirely new principle. From the services point of view, it had two advantages over all other pens; it could be taken to any height without leaking, and it would also write under water. Airmen and frogmen, for instance, would obviously find it invaluable.

I examined this marvel thoroughly. Outwardly it resembled the old stylo pen, but on taking it to pieces, I discovered that at the writing end was a tiny ball-bearing which revolved as it moved over the writing surface. A specially oiled ink was fed on to the metal ball from a narrow tube.

'It's tremendous, Clutty!' enthused my friend. 'We've tried it in the air and under water. It's passed every test with flying colours. These things are the answer to so many of our problems that I'd like to issue one to every operational flier. Now, you've got all sorts of useful connections in various factories. Do you think you could arrange for the immediate production of, say, ten thousand pens, regardless of cost?'

'I fancy so,' I replied, 'but I'd like to meet the inventor first and have a chat with him. What's his name?'

'Henry Martin.'

'And his address?'

'I believe he's staying at the Argentine Club in Piccadilly.'

After thanking my friend for the information, I pocketed the prototype and set out to call on the ingenious Mr Martin.

My luck was in. I located the gentleman in the club lounge, showed him his pen by way of introduction and explained how I had been drawn into the affair. I demonstrated the uses of one of our escape pens to let him know that we shared a common interest, and then asked him if he had taken any action to commercialize his invention.

'Well, I have and I haven't,' said Martin slowly. 'I certainly intended to and then I changed my mind. It's a long story. I suppose it all goes back to the first year of the war, when a man walked into my office in Buenos Aires and tried to interest me in a roughly made model of what I now call the ball-point pen. He assured me he was Swiss, but I had a shrewd suspicion he was one of those Germans who got out after Hitler assumed power. Might very well have been a German Jew. Anyway, one look at his invention convinced me that, with certain minor modifications, it was a winner, so we came to terms about it and I agreed to provide the cash that was necessary to produce the perfect pen.'

'You were in Buenos Aires, you say?'

'That's right. My two brothers and I – we're all three accountants – emigrated to South Africa after the first World War, but nothing went right for us, so we decided to try our fortunes in South America. Fate was kinder to us there and within a few years we had established an accountancy business to be proud of. It was then that I started to invest in a number of private enterprises. I suppose that's how the pseudo-Swiss fellow got to hear about me.'

'I'm surprised you didn't launch the pen in the United States.'

'I probably would have done, if it hadn't been for the war,' Martin replied. 'You see, Major, although I'd been away for a long time, I still had a soft spot for the Old Country. I guess it's not easy to stop being an Englishman. In an odd way I felt that the ball-point pen might have some military value. So instead of exploiting the American market, I parcelled up half a dozen pens and despatched them by diplomatic bag to the Foreign Office.' He paused, his face set in sombre lines, and then went on, 'I waited for six months, but I heard nothing – not even an acknowledgment. It was heart-breaking. I was so disgusted that I went straight round to the American Embassy in Buenos Aires and showed them the pen in confidence. A few days later, the US Government sent an aircraft to collect me and take me to Washington, and believe it or not, the authorities had already lined up one of the big pen-making corporations. All I had to do was to sign on the dotted line, sit back and enjoy millions of dollars in royalties for the rest of my life.'

I gazed in awe at this incredible man. 'And you didn't sign?'

'No, I did not. I still had the quixotic notion that England should have the pen first. I left the Americans dangling and visited the British Embassy in Washington. For once our people swung into action. Twenty-four hours after I had demonstrated the advantages of the ball-point, I found myself in a bomber *en route* for London. My first port of call was the Foreign Office. Exhaustive inquiries finally produced the shame-faced admission that my pens had been pushed into a cupboard and forgotten. I spent a refreshing five minutes telling the individual responsible exactly what I thought of him, stormed out, and as a last desperate gesture, forwarded a couple of pens to each of the three services. As you know, the RAF has made the first move. I understand ten thousand are wanted to begin with, but owing to wartime controls, there's very little that can be done.'

I hastened to inform Mr Martin that a great deal could be done and that I would personally guarantee a delivery of ten thousand ball-point pens to the RAF in less than a month's time. He wished me every success, asked me to keep him in the picture with regard to future developments and said he would support me no matter what happened.

From the Argentine Club I shot off to the factory that had long been producing our escape pens. I swore the manager to secrecy, handed him a sample pen and told him I required ten thousand as soon as possible. To spur him on, I mentioned that if the RAF order was satisfactorily met, the inventor of the pen might be persuaded to let the company manufacture ball-points for the general public at a later date. Impressing upon him the importance of keeping his mouth shut about the transaction, I took my leave, and well content with my day's work, returned to our country headquarters.

The day after I had visited him, however, my telephone rang, and on lifting the instrument, I heard a cold official voice invite me to attend an interview at a certain room in the War Office. I recognized the room number. I was wanted by MI 5.

That same afternoon, Jill drove me to town and I made my way to the security department of the War Office. Although the two men who received me were dressed in civilian clothes, I could see at a glance that they were typical products of New Scotland Yard. One of them, who sat behind a desk facing me, waved me to a chair. His opening question was fired at me in the clipped authoritative accents detectives seem to cultivate.

'Are you working for any Government department, sir?'

'I am.'

'Which department?'

'That's my affair,' I countered. 'Why are you questioning me?'

'We're conducting an investigation on behalf of the Director of Public Prosecutions,' was the pompous reply. 'And it has come to our notice that – '

'Listen,' I cut in quickly. 'I know exactly what's worrying you. You're barking up the wrong tree. Get rid of your stooge and I'll tell you a few things that will save you making an utter fool of yourself.'

My interrogator's face darkened, but he knew I meant what I said. He glanced across at his henchman and gave an almost imperceptible nod. The second detective annihilated me with a look and stalked out.

As soon as we were alone, I produced my credentials, told him how I came to be connected with the ball-point pen deal and satisfied him that I had simply been trying to help the RAF. Reducing the affair to its essentials, I made it clear to him that any probing into my activities was tantamount to snooping on the Air Ministry. If I had attempted to short-circuit the official supply system, I added, it had been because the Royal Air Force had needed the pens in a hurry. Emergency conditions had demanded emergency measures. My sole aim had been to get ten thousand pens without undue delay.

After the detective had apologized for the inconvenience he had caused me, I popped across to the Air

Ministry to tell my friend what had happened. Under the circumstances he decided reluctantly to proceed no further with the business, and so, for the rest of the war, high-flying airmen were obliged to use pens that spluttered and leaked, with the inevitable result that log book entries made above a certain altitude were largely indecipherable.

Henry Martin, his patriotism shaken by the bureaucrats, then pursued his own course, and eventually the Miles Aircraft Co. manufactured his pen with huge success.

11　The Other Side

In case I have inadvertently left the reader with the impression that our enemies were either stupid or blind, I should like to state quite categorically that those Germans who were responsible for running the prisoner-of-war camps were intelligent, shrewd and painstaking men, and that *in time* they intercepted nearly all of my various gadgets. The point was that each new device served its turn for a while and was of considerable benefit to escapers, but once it was 'blown', we either modified it or abandoned it altogether. When the camp searchers hit on the secret of our button compass, for example, we fooled them for an additional period by manufacturing it with a left-hand thread. Any attempt to unscrew it, therefore, only tightened the thing. It was as simple as that.

It follows, then, that if the camp censors gradually came to nullify the effectiveness of every trick I played on them, by the end of the war the German security experts must have been in possession of the full story of my inventions, of my smuggling techniques and of the different communication systems I employed. In short, by the time Germany was defeated, all the information contained in this present volume must have been collected together in a file in Berlin. The Russians had access to that file; so did the French, the Belgians, the Dutch, the Italians and everybody else who was in at the kill. I have not mentioned the Americans, because I had already given them samples of all my 'toys'.

Moreover, since the war, newspaper articles and a spate of escape books have covered every possible angle of our department's contribution to the war effort. In fact, I have a batch of press cuttings in which are detailed references to all the contrivances I provided for the use of escapers, evaders and Resistance people.

If I seem to be labouring these points, it is because I also wish to make it clear that in compiling this record of my special wartime work, I am not giving away any secrets. A secret, by definition, is something kept private, not made known or exposed to view. Newspapers and books are read by a wide public. Escape gadgets and escape methods therein described can no longer be treated as *arcana*.

The material that follows, then, is submitted as evidence that the tale I have told contains no breach of security. The Germans found out what we were doing in every instance, but by the time they had blocked our pipe-line, we had already laid another. They were smart, but we were smarter.

First of all, I quote almost the whole of a letter I received some years after the war from Baron von Lindeiner, former Commandant of Stalag Luft III. These are the observations of a man who studied our methods from the other side of the wire.

'During the last war,' von Lindeiner writes, 'as I spoke English fluently and was one of the more elderly officers of the German forces, I was made Commandant of one of the more important prisoner-of-war camps.

'In our early days, before the British and United States air forces grew to their great size, we did not have many inmates, but it became evident to all camp commandants even then that we were going to have a lot of trouble from these youthful fliers, and it was not long before we realized that every one of them had been told it was their duty to escape from their prison confines. At the beginning of the war, with few prisoners to interrogate and examine, we soon came to understand that a huge scheme was officially behind the efforts of the fliers to help them escape. Of course, none of the camp staffs in those days had sufficient evidence to estimate how big the enemy scheme was. It was only later on, as the war dragged along, that the immensity of the scheme became evident.

'I have heard since the war ended that the general opinion of German camp commandants was that they were all a lot of hard-hearted men with no sense of humour, but this was not altogether true. Many of us had a great sense of humour and treated the "devilment" of the young fliers in a not entirely serious manner, at the same time carrying out our duty to our own forces in trying to prevent escapes taking place.

'This might at first thought seem an easy thing to have done. It was far from easy, believe me. It must be remembered that the time soon came when the prisoners far outnumbered the guards, and thus the problem became a nightmare to us. Whilst our guards were naturally "on their toes", so were the prisoners, each and every one of them.

'They were always pitting their brains against our camp systems, more or less on the lines of each man being an individual magician working out a trick to escape. This meant that in the camps we were faced with a lot of brainy young conjurors who had plenty of time in which to work out their various tricks against us.

'In those first few months we soon acquired evidence of what was going on, because after the fliers came into the camps, they were searched and found to have upon their persons the most ingenious equipment, much of which was standardized. This included very clever silk maps secreted in their clothing. As they were printed on silk, the maps made no noise during a search. Moreover, each flier was given a most useful ration box, which in itself was a whole bag of tricks. Compasses of many types were discovered, so small that many slipped through a search undetected. Some of those concealed in tunic buttons were perfectly made.

'We had no doubt that the wicked British were behind this vast scheme, because when the American fliers came down later in the war, and eventually found their way into the camps as prisoners, they too were equipped with exactly the same type of escape material.

'Shortly after their arrival, the inmates began to get busy inside the camps on their own account. They soon became expert forgers of passes and of other necessary documents required on a journey through Germany by any who got out. At this work many ingenious ideas were put into practice.

'However vigilant our guards were, it was only with the greatest difficulty that many of these schemes were brought to light. It was quite impossible to watch every prisoner night and day. Our work in the camps was made even more arduous owing to the vast amount of "smuggled" goods introduced into parcels sent from England by the British organization responsible. I must admit that at no time during the whole war was a parcel from the Red Cross ever found to contain anything other than official items. All the "smuggled" goods were sent to prisoners in what to us appeared to be quite innocent packages, sent in the guise of welfare bundles from various societies and charity funds.

'This fraud was extremely well carried out, but nevertheless as each new society started to send parcels, our search staffs examined them and at last located the different escape aids that were inside the parcels. Our trouble was, however, that many parcels got through first, before we uncovered the scheme. Furthermore, only a few parcels in each batch from any one society contained material which, according to our camp laws, was illegal.

'Two of the most ingenious aids that I personally found were the very clever uniforms that came into the camps and quantities of German money skilfully pressed into gramophone records. The uniforms were perfectly made and with very little alteration could be transformed into German military wear. The total amount of illegal material sent in this way must have been considerable.

'The prisoners themselves manufactured such highly efficient gear as wireless sets, each set taking many months of labour to produce.

'It is not surprising that towards the end of the war, supported by all this help from home, many prisoners managed to escape and get back to England. Then again, the number that got back home was nothing compared to the huge number that escaped and were duly caught again, thus causing us enormous trouble in the camps.

'When the prisoners were eventually caught, they were usually given a spell of solitary confinement, but I believe that not one of them could ever say that we punished them too harshly. As soon as they were returned to the main camp, we had no doubt that they were up to their fun and games again.'

So much for the opinions expressed by Baron von Lindeiner, ex-Commandant of Stalag Luft III.

And here is the opinion of one of the actual camp guards.

October 12th, 1955

Dear Mr Hutton,

On the occasion of a recent visit I paid to a friend of mine in Berlin – Herr Meisel, who served some time with the Verband Deutscher Soldaten e.V., – I heard that you would like to know how the German guards in prisoner-of-war camps were constantly fooled by the British methods of sending parcels, which appeared to be innocent, but in fact were far from innocent.

Although I was over 50 when the last war started, being a technical man (I was in the telephone department of the German Post Office) and also speaking fairly good English, I was drafted into the Army Signal Corps and posted to a section dealing with field telephones. Early in 1940 I was badly wounded in action near Liége; in hospital, to save my life, they had to amputate my right leg.

Early in 1941 I was posted as a guard to several prisoner camps, and was eventually posted to Oflag VII C. To begin with I was just an ordinary guard, but since my injury made it impossible for me to stand for a long period, I asked the camp commandant to give me some more useful work so that I would not have to stay on my feet too long. Eventually I was posted to the parcels department of the camp; other guards were already working here, but I had the advantage of my knowledge of English and French.

As the war proceeded, incoming prisoners increased all the time and their accommodation became a real problem; naturally the number of parcels arriving increased in proportion. The British prisoners gave us more trouble than other nationals, chiefly because the majority were mad on sport and gymnastics (we Germans are the same). On account of this, many of the British devices got through to the British prisoners hidden in sporting equipment, before they were discovered.

When suspicion was aroused, it was only natural to think that much of this contraband was arriving in Red Cross bundles, and much time was wasted in the careful but fruitless examination of large numbers of parcels. Often our examining X-ray apparatus broke down and we were unable to get replacements from Berlin as they were all being sent to the front. The result was that vast numbers of parcels were held up for examination and the prisoners became violently insulting to us all, threatening to report these hold-ups to the Swiss Government. This they did, and we were ordered by our superiors in Berlin to release large blocks of the held-up parcels, which of course were never examined. In such cases much escape material must have reached the prisoners, to our great annoyance.

I have very good reason to remember all this, because by order of Berlin many of the parcels guards were put under arrest for failing in their duty to discover this contraband material. This was most unjust, for not we but our superiors should have been punished – in particular those Gestapo people from Berlin who kept on lecturing us but never gave any real help in solving the problem.

I think it was about the middle of 1942 that we suddenly realized that the British authorities must have organized a huge transit of bogus parcels. But as these bogus bundles came with identical parcels, which did not seem to contain anything improper and far exceeded those containing illegal material, our work in examination was considerably wasted.

I remember an enormous number of parcels arriving over many months, which were forwarded from 'The Brewers' Society of Great Britain'. Hundreds of these must have infiltrated into other compounds as well as my own. In them was an enormous board, some two feet long, with lines marked across it and small metal coins. This was some type of British game which we found hard to understand, but it seemed to amuse the British prisoners for hours on end. In my compound, I think it was nearly six months before we discovered that a tremendous amount of escape material, such as compasses, money, ink, maps, wire and many other dangerous items, was hidden in these peculiar games.

As these parcels also contained such things as

blankets, boots, socks, undergarments, hats etc., which were quite legitimate, examination made our work far more difficult.

Some of the discoveries we made were accidental. I remember for instance seeing with one of our officers a piece of string hanging from a window. When we found the room it hung from we discovered that the string was attached to a wireless set as an aerial. Puzzled by this, we examined the string and found that it had a strong wire as its centre. The string had been used on an enormous number of parcels, yet from that time not all the string we examined seemed to contain wire.

Of course towards the end of the war, as we Germans became extremely short of food, unfortunately much bribery was discovered among the German guards – particularly those who lived outside the camps. This was due to the British being very well supplied with such foods as butter, cocoa, tea, coffee and sweets in their parcels, and also by contraband parcels bought with German money. The prisoners were thus able to exchange such precious foods for wireless tubes, railway maps, ration cards and other valuables.

At that time the guards were blamed for anything that went wrong, but in fairness to them I must say that as things began to get worse towards the end of the war, it was not only the guards who suffered, but their families, too.

This of course did not apply to the higher strata in military or civil circles, which later brought about their own undoing.

I hope that you will find all this useful.

(signed)

H. GOEHR

Although it would appear that the memory of the guard who wrote the above has played him false, none the less the simplicity of our scheme seems to have worked – as the letter opposite will show.

LICENSED VICTUALLERS SPORTS ASSOCIATION

(WHOLESALE ONLY)

Telephone	10, St. Bride Street,	Secretary
Central 6952	London E.C.4.	J. H. Sherwell

SUPPLIERS OF GAMES AND BAR REQUISITES TO HOTELS. RESTAURANTS. SPORTS CLUBS AND OTHER LICENSED PREMISES

12th May, 1941.

Dear Sir,

Owing to the difficulties in the present situation of obtaining new supplies of sporting goods used in our various Public Houses, Inns, etc., it has been decided by the Association to suspend for the duration of the war our activities in this direction.

Your name has been published as a prisoner of war, and our committee feel that no better purpose can be found for the use of our present stock of goods, than to distribute them to those unfortunate members of the services who are at present in prisoner of war camps.

Accordingly we are despatching to you a parcel of these goods which we hope will reach you in due course in good condition and that you and your colleagues will find them of use.

Should this parcel reach you, your acknowledgement to us would be welcome.

Yours faithfully,

J. H. Sherwell

Secretary.

ACKNOWLEDGEMENT

KRIEGSGEFANGENENPOST

The Secretary
LICENSED VICTUALLERS
SPORTS ASSOCIATION
10 St. Bride Street,
London, E.C.4.

Date. 20th August, '41

Parcel No.   14361   Containing

5 Records.
1 Dart Board.
1 Chess Set.
1 Shovehalfpenny Board.

has been received by me.

(sgd) J. Short,
Major.

```
Geprüft
24
Oflag IXA
```

Finally, I should like to draw the reader's attention to the following extracts from a dossier of German military appreciations, put together by a High Court Judge of the American Supreme Court whilst attending the Nuremberg trials.

The following particular accounts show the many-sided and skilled preparations of the Royal Air Force in order to enable their personnel to escape, in case of baling out of their machines or through forced landings on enemy territory, and to return to their units.

The present report has to give to the organization of ground personnel of the German Air Force and to all services charged to arrest and watch enemy Air Force prisoners, a survey of the means of escape with which enemy fliers are equipped, in order to enable them to take efficient counter-measures. Any new means of escape discovered is to be sent in to the nearest unit immediately.

An examination of the clothes belonging to the crews of Anglo-American planes shows that these have been provided in a very clever manner with all sorts of aids to escape. Their abundance and variety prove that the enemy set a great value on the return of their flying personnel. The chief motive is probably the long and expensive training given to members of flying crews, which represent the best qualified forces of the British and American nations.

Repeatedly successful break-outs by Englishmen have probably convinced enemy Governments of the rightness of their proceedings in helping their men escape. Therefore they have made it the duty of all soldiers and airmen to escape as stated in an order to the X Squadron. The literal translation of the order runs thus: 'Every member of the United States Army is obliged to avoid capture by the enemy, or if captured, he must escape. The same rule applies to members of the RAF.'

The following information, supported by illustrations, surveys the many means of assistance with which the flying personnel of the Royal Air Force are provided and of the way these materials are camouflaged in their clothes. As the same things are found continually on thousands of prisoners, it is probable that almost the entire flying cadre is provided with machine-made means of escape as part of the regulation equipment.

Preceding the start of a raid, the first and second crew chiefs receive from their unit an army bag, which contains the escape material for the whole crew. The first step in the scheme for escape assistance is the issue of passport photographs. Every member of the crew receives two passport photographs taken in civilian clothes, which he must constantly keep in his possession. If a plane is shot down over enemy territory, every member of the crew must try to reach one of the secret escape organizations in the occupied countries.

Among other items is the emergency provision parcel. This helps the fugitive to travel for several days without asking for assistance from the civilian population. It is a stiff celluloid transparent parcel, waterproof, and in it, neatly arranged and skilfully folded, are the following:

> 2 rolls of sticking plaster; 4 benzedrine tablets; 12 halazone tablets; 23 Horlick's tablets; 8 chewing-gum tablets; 1 rubber bag for water; 1 box of matches; 1 flat compass; 1 sewing box (tube) with 2 needles and thread.

Another means of escape is the money-bag, containing in foreign currency bank-notes as follows:

1,000 French francs; 350 Belgian francs; 20
Dutch guilders.

The crew likewise receive maps for quick and efficient reading, and the money-bags usually contain
three maps each. Maps are hidden in the lining of the
bag, which is roughly 5 inches by 4 inches. The maps
are made of very thin silk and are folded far more
easily than the thin paper ones. They do not crease
as the paper ones do. The printing on the paper maps
becomes illegible after many foldings. These maps
are remarkable for their clarity and completeness.
The following list shows the scale of each map:

German-Swiss frontier	1 : 300,000
SW France and Spain	1 : 1,000,000
Pyrenees, East, West and Middle	1 : 500,000
NW France, Belgium, Holland	1 : 1,000,000
France, Germany, Switzerland	1 : 3,000,000
Portugal, Spain	1 : 1,000,000
Spain, France	1 : 1,000,000
Belgium, Germany	1 : 250,000
Holland, Belgium, France, West Germany	1 : 1,000,000

Each of these forms part of one complete map and
the following items are marked with great clarity:

Frontiers; Forbidden areas − near frontiers;
Demarcation line with France; Former French
frontier.

The maps are superbly marked in miles and kilo-
metres, and the mountains near the frontiers show
the exact heights and all passes.

Examinations also show that bank-notes have been
inserted in the shoes of the fliers. Half-shoes, as
shown in the illustration, have money hidden under
a thin leather lining over the heel. Bank-notes have

been found concealed in electrically heated gloves, hidden in the lining in such a careful manner that damage is avoided.

The 'escape bag' also contains the following item: a compass, small and round. It is of simple but perfect construction and is very suitable for rough working out of escape routes quickly.

The following items have been found:

Compass in uniform button. If the top of this button is turned to the left, the two halves will separate. One part contains a compass.

Trouser button compass. Two flat lacquered buttons of different metals are used for this. One button is magnetized and works on top of the other.

Flat compasses in seal rings. These seem to be used only by United States air crews. It would seem that members of crews buy these in their own country while training.

Pendulum compass. Prisoners carry a piece of bar-metal, magnetized, which swings due north when hung on a length of thread.

Compass in tobacco pipe. This is most ingenious in that the pipe can be used. The mouthpiece contains an extremely tiny compass, protected by rubber.

Pencil compass. Lately wooden pencils have been found containing bar compasses. The pencil must be broken at a point indicated by a certain letter in the maker's name.

Escape saw. There are many of these in different forms. They are about five inches long, of leaf steel, half an inch wide and very thin, with great sawing power. Some have saws on one edge; others on both.

A careful study of all this shows that the enemy has provided for all his flying crews every possible help for an immediate escape. This does not only refer to financial aid, but to all the separate and numerous items of equipment herein listed, plus other devices which will be the subject of a further report. It must be conceded that our enemy works hard to provide constantly so many new additions to escape material.

It is worth noting that the Germans did not complete their investigations into the work of our escape department until the end of 1944. By that time, of course, there was little need to call upon the services of our organization. Most of the prisoners being taken at that stage of the war were Germans.

12   Baby-Face and the Contortionist

I feel sure my American readers will wonder how many prisoners of war actually reached home to safety. The answer is complex, but obviously, for reasons of security, I cannot mention numbers. I must emphasize, though, that it was not only those brave men who actually returned home 'under their own steam' who confounded the enemy. In many cases prisoners caused German camp authorities no end of trouble by breaking out of camps, even though knowing full well they would probably be caught quickly and thrust into the 'cooler' when picked up and returned.

By way of illustrating how two escapers actually did manage to get home, I have chosen two incidents: one, at the end of which I was presented with one of my favourite escape gadgets, and the other, which ended with a theatrical flourish that appealed to my sense of showmanship. In both cases I have used fictitious names for my heroes, as they may one day decide to add full accounts of their experiences to the growing body of escape literature. But the stories are authentic and I have included them in order to correct any disproportionate impression I may have given by concentrating overmuch on the part we played in the escape business. When all is said and done, no matter how extensive our assistance may have been, no prisoner could have achieved his liberty without courage, patience, ingenuity and downright pertinacity—those qualities in a man which are worth more than a million clever contraptions. Our bits and pieces helped, but ninety-nine per cent of the credit for any escape goes to the man who carried it out.

Lieutenant Sand, or Baby-Face—twenty-two, good-looking, well-groomed—was among the unlucky ones who were left behind after the Dunkirk evacuation. He was a Scot, ambitious, and immensely proud of his regiment. It so happened that his unit was one of the few that I had been able to equip with the button compass. He had heard of my peculiar wares and had paid me a personal visit on his embarkation leave. I liked him—he reminded me of my own son—and I was delighted to help him.

It was some months after the Dunkirk disaster that I learned he was a prisoner-of-war in a camp near Dresden. I wondered at the time if he would attempt an escape, but in view of the reports we had of German security measures, I was not oversanguine.

Sand, however, was not the type of man to accept captivity with a philosophic shrug. Despite the apparently insuperable barriers that lay between the prisoner and liberty, he was determined right from the start to get out.

In accordance with correct procedure, he informed the senior British officer in the camp of his intentions, but admitted that he had no definite plans at that stage. He had examined all possible points of egress—cell windows, floors, roofs, passages, perimeter wire. He had been forced to the reluctant conclusion that he would have to wait and seize whatever favourable opportunity the future might provide. In the meantime, he had his compass button and access to one of our silk maps of Germany.

He hung on hopefully, biding his time and praying for a change in the normal daily routine. He occupied himself in making a civilian suit from such oddments as he was able to collect. Using a homemade dye, he transformed the crazy patchwork into one uniform colour and was satisfied that his clothes would get by any casual inspection. He also started to make a careful copy of the escape map on thin sheets of toilet paper. He could have had the original, but he was too considerate to deprive his fellow prisoners of one of the few silk maps available in the camp.

Then came the news that more prisoners were expected. The camp would have to be enlarged to accommodate them. Pretending that the ground was to be used for the growing of additional vegetables for the prisoners, the Germans invited their captives to help in clearing a vast area outside the camp perimeter. Volunteers were immediately forthcoming, for the men saw in the task a welcome break in the day-to-day monotony as well as a daily jaunt outside the wire. Needless to say, Lieutenant Sand was one of the first to join this working-party. Bearing spades, picks, axes and saws, and escorted by armed guards, the men would tramp to a tract of scrubland and spend a few hours each day preparing the ground where the new barracks were to be erected. At the end of their labours they would return to camp under the watchful eyes of the guards, and the gates would again be locked behind them. They all found their little excursion a pleasant diversion. Lieutenant Sand found it most enlightening.

On leaving the camp they were lined up and counted. There was no check on the return journey.

As the days passed the terrain was gradually cleared of trees and bushes, and the 'agricultural' party asked the senior German N.C.O. for permission to kick a football about on the patch they had already levelled. He consented at once, so on the following day one of the party took along a football and at the end of their shift, the men enjoyed a short recreational period.

Autumn came and shorter days, and the prisoners were ordered to dig a drainage trench around the perimeter.

Hedges were also to be planted to mark the boundaries. When the day's digging was completed, the men played football until dusk and then set off on the trek back to the main camp.

Lieutenant Sand decided that the circumstances were admirable for his break. The weather experts in the camp informed him that he could expect dry weather for some days to come. He had saved up part of his rations over a period. He had his button compass, his map and his civilian suit. But he had no money and his knowledge of German was limited to the words and phrases he had picked up from daily contact with the camp staff. His chances, everybody thought, were slight.

But on the day he selected for his attempt, Sand was full of confidence. He donned his civilian suit under his uniform, pinning a beret to it before setting out for the afternoon's digging session. By previous arrangement, he carried the football.

Digging finished at 5.30 P.M. From then until six the men booted the ball about, laughing and joking as usual and surreptitiously wishing young Sand the best of luck on his forthcoming venture. The shadows were closing in as they formed up near one of the trenches preparatory to marching off. Sand, who had taken charge of the football, was tossing it up and down idly, when suddenly he contrived to drop it so that it rolled away from the shallow trench. With distracting whoops and yells, the rest of the party charged for it. The guards—there were four of them altogether—joined in the mad pursuit.

Like an arrow from a bow, Lieutenant Sand streaked for the excavations, dived in headlong and lay there motionless. He heard his comrades' shouts and shrieks, the barked commands of the German guards, the rhythmic tramp of feet fading away into the distance, and then—

silence. By that time his heartbeats were back to normal and his initial terror had abated.

He made no move until nightfall. He knew with disturbing certitude that he would be missed at the nine o'clock roll call. He would have to get as far as possible from the area before the alarm was sounded.

He swiftly shed his uniform and, after removing one precious button, buried the tunic and trousers in the ditch. He donned his beret and, guided by his tiny compass, headed across country in a southwesterly direction. He knew exactly where he was heading. He remembered that he had been told in lectures of that curious section of Switzerland that juts out into Germany and through which Johnny Evans had escaped in the First World War —the Schaffhausen salient. He would emulate Evans and cross into Switzerland by that tried and tested route. His toilet-paper map would show him which towns to avoid on his zigzag journey through Lower Saxony, across the Jura and into Wurttemberg. As a boy he had often dreamed of walking beside the Danube. Before his trip ended, that was precisely what he would be doing.

Incredible though it may sound, this plucky young man covered the whole of his four-hundred-mile journey on foot, most of it over rough country twelve hundred feet above sea level. He used roads only when he had to and invariably at night. He swam streams and rivers, slept out in the open, and, when his food reserve was exhausted, subsisted on whatever he could scrounge from fields. For twenty-seven days he plodded across southern Germany. On the twenty-eighth he was nearly caught when only eight miles from the Swiss frontier.

He had been resting in the corner of a field when he foolishly did something he had been warned never to do as an escaper. It was his first mistake and it might have

cost him dear. He spotted a signpost on the far side of
the hedge that was sheltering him from the road, and
thinking there was nobody about, stepped out to the roadway to have a closer look at it and to check his position.

Before he could move, a German soldier suddenly appeared on a bicycle, dismounted and asked a question
Sand did not understand.

Unhesitatingly Sand charged the bewildered soldier and
knocked him off balance with his bicycle on top of him.
In falling, the fellow hit his head on a large stone and lay
there for a moment partly stunned. Sand leaped on him
and ruthlessly cracked the soldier's head on the stone a
second time. He then picked up the bicycle, which
fortunately had not been damaged, sprang on to the saddle
and pedalled furiously down the road towards the frontier.

He travelled in this manner for six miles, meeting
nobody. At a bridge over a river he halted, pitched the
bicycle into the waters below, and proceeded along the
bank on foot, intending to find a quiet spot in which to
hide until nightfall. At last he struck suitable cover and
curled up among a heap of boulders. In the few hours of
daylight that remained, he plotted his position with map
and compass and then waited until darkness fell. When
he judged it was safe, he crawled along the river bank for
more than a mile.

If his calculations were correct, he was somewhere
inside the Schaffhausen salient. The danger was to continue too far. It was only too easy to traverse the salient
and to cross over into Germany once more.

Sand advanced cautiously until he reached a railway
viaduct. He froze in his tracks when he heard what he
thought was German being spoken. After an appreciable
interval he edged forward along a ditch. He had the fright
of his life when suddenly he was challenged from behind.

But the challenge had been issued in French. He was over the border and in neutral territory.

The kindly Swiss whisked him away to a hospital, there to recover from the effects of his gruelling trek. He could afford to smile when he was told that it had indeed been a German voice which had startled him and that at the time he had been a mere thirty yards inside the salient. He had heard the German sentry calling to his relief at the frontier post.

My first intimation that Sand had been repatriated came when he strolled into my office and holding out his hand, said, 'I thought you might care to have this as a souvenir of at least one prisoner who got back with its aid.'

Lying in the centre of his outstretched palm was my button compass. . . .

I must preface my second escape story by saying that as the war progressed and my own particular work expanded, I obtained most of my office fittings—lamps, extra chairs, carpets, curtains—by employing the old-fashioned barter principle. One of my strongest supporters in this highly irregular system was also a veteran of the First World War. He had an office quite near my own and as it was his business to distribute, among other things, those attractive items that can transform a dismally barren room into a luxuriously appointed office, I set a great deal of value upon the friendship that had sprung between us. The apple of his eye was undoubtedly his son, a regular officer in the R.A.F., a magnificent bomber pilot and almost as tall and thin as a lamp-post. For the purposes of this narrative I shall call him Tallboy.

For six months this brilliant youngster had been 'softening up' enemy targets night after night in his Wellington. Then Providence deserted him on a return trip by moonlight. His aircraft was so badly damaged by flakage that he and the crew were obliged to bale out. He floated down and landed in a shallow river, not far from the bank. He thought at first that he was in Holland, but then found to his chagrin that he was inside Germany, although only a couple of miles from the Dutch frontier. He rested awhile to recover his spirits and then set off towards the German-Dutch border, walking in the water in case blood-hounds were set on his track.

At last he emerged from the river and made a dash for the Control Post. By sheer bad luck, as soon as he set foot on the road, he ran smack into a German patrol. He was captured and eventually imprisoned in a new camp near Stuttgart.

He reported to the senior British officer and seemed to settle down, although he kept to himself, saying little and not mixing with his fellow prisoners. For hours at a time he would sit apart from the others, quietly contemplating his surroundings, brooding, paying scant attention to the multifarious activities of his companions in misfortune. Because of his unsociable habits he became known as the 'Recluse.'

His comrades did not know it, but, like Lieutenant Sand, Tallboy was concentrating wholly on the problem of escape.

He watched everything that was going on, mentally recording all aspects of the monotonous camp routine, waiting patiently for a feasible break-out plan to suggest itself. The days passed slowly, but Tallboy was gradually groping his way towards the realization of his dreams. He had noticed, for instance, that all rubbish was stuffed into extraordinarily large Hessian sacks, which hung on the walls of the barrack huts. When the sacks were full, the Germans collected them and dumped them on the back of an open lorry. This vehicle was then driven from the compound to a huge refuse heap within sight of the camp. There the bulging sacks were added to the enormous stack of refuse. The scavenging party never emptied the contents. Either the sacks were plentiful or the Germans thought it more hygienic to leave the litter unexposed.

Tallboy then began to practise what the other prisoners assumed was a peculiar form of yoga. He would double himself up like a jackknife and sit with his feet behind his neck in the manner of a contortionist. At first he could hold this unconventional pose for only a minute. He improved on this time with every day that passed, until he could remain in his curious posture for as long as two hours.

When he was not tying himself up in knots, he was busy preparing his clothing for the forthcoming escape. He gathered together sufficient remnants to make for himself a German labourer's suit and a poke hat. Under the lapel of the jacket he fastened a razor blade. Next, he altered his service greatcoat and dyed it an indeterminate shade of brown. He felt confident that if only he could get outside the wire, he would be able to pass himself off as a typical working-man, especially in a country where ersatz suits were the rule rather than the exception.

Such was Tallboy's singleness of purpose that he spent nine months preparing for his escape-attempt. Little by little he accumulated a reserve of food that he hoped would be adequate for the seven-hundred-mile stretch that lay between him and the port he proposed to aim for—Danzig. He had carefully weighed the possibilities of either hiking across the rugged Jura or travelling in a wide arc through the edge of the Black Forest, with the Schaffhausen salient as his ultimate objective. Both routes had their attractions—less than a hundred miles of march and a neutral country beckoning—but Tallboy suspected that the Germans would also appreciate their obvious appeal. As soon as his absence was discovered, search parties would be dispatched immediately to those very regions. With Switzerland a mere three or four days' foot-slogging away, they would think it unlikely that an escaper would deliberately choose to penetrate even farther into Germany. The extra six hundred miles would be tough going, but if he foxed the enemy, they would be well worth the effort.

Our modest contribution to Tallboy's accessories was threefold. He had our compass, our silk map, and a small amount of German currency. Not very much, perhaps, and as it turned out, one of the items proved unnecessary, but nevertheless, the very fact that he had them was of considerable morale value. He was not entirely naked to his enemies.

Dressed in his civilian clothes, with his food and his escape aids concealed about his person, this remarkable young man adopted his yogi's attitude for the last time. His friends in the barrack hut lifted him up, bent double as he was, with his feet locked behind his neck, and lowered him into the long Hessian rubbish sack. Crumpled sheets of paper were wedged around him to camouflage his shape, and on top of him went more litter and a few empty cans.

Half an hour later the German sanitation squad came for the sack. One of them humped it on his back, staggered to the waiting lorry and flung it across the tailboard—a performance which the other prisoners watched with bated breath. More sacks were collected and the truck was driven through the gates towards the dumping ground. The load was disposed of in the usual manner, the vehicle made a U-turn and roared off in the direction of the camp.

Tallboy, grotesquely enthroned on the rubbish heap, was outside the wire.

Now began an agonizing period for the amateur contortionist. He relaxed as best he could in the confined space and resigned himself to three hours of near suffocation until darkness fell. When daylight ceased to filter through his canvas cocoon, he groped for the razor blade, slit the sack lengthwise, and wriggled out. For some time he lay there on his back, gingerly exercising his legs until circulation was fully restored. In the distance he could see the lights of his former prison. He knew that roll call was not far off.

On hands and knees he crawled across the fields to a minor road, and there he had a real stroke of luck. Only a few yards away, leaning up against a tree outside an inn, was a bicycle. Tallboy tiptoed towards it, sprang on to the saddle and glided silently away in a north-easterly direction.

At first light he hid in the dense woods not far from the Neckar, remaining under cover throughout the whole of that day. In the evening he moved on again, steering vaguely towards Plauen. Travelling only at night, he pushed steadily on until, as dawn was breaking on the fifth day, he reached a fairly big railway junction. He pedalled into the country for about half a mile, sank under a hedge bordering a convenient field and studied his map. All the signs indicated that he could count on trains running from the junction direct to Danzig.

Tallboy, infinitely patient, hung on till nightfall.

Heavy clouds veiled the face of the moon when he scrambled to his feet and, abandoning his bicycle, crept down to the railway yard and dived in among the long lines of wagons. He watched several goods trains come in and pull out. He inspected the truck labels eagerly, but none of them bore the wished-for name: Danzig. Utterly exhausted, he crawled under a tarpaulin protecting a stack of paint drums, stretched himself out gratefully, and fell asleep.

Shivering, cramped and profoundly miserable, he emerged from his hide-out at four o'clock in the morning. Another goods train had arrived during the night and had clanked to a standstill only a dozen yards away without waking him. The station yard seemed deserted. Cautiously he made his way to the nearest wagon and peered at the label – Danzig.

Ninety-nine men out of a hundred would have clambered into the open wagon, curled up in a corner and hoped for the best. Tallboy was the hundredth man. He wriggled underneath and found that he could hold on to the under-carriage with his hands and feet. It would be an uncomfortable way to travel, but with support of some kind, he believed he could endure it. He knew instinctively that safety lay in avoiding the obvious.

He scuttled back to the tarpaulin and prowled around the drums, searching frantically for a length of rope. He saw none, but he did manage to unearth a coil of wire in a small shed. He returned to the wagon, wormed his way back to the understructure and wired himself to the tangle of metal rods and projections. He had not been there long when the train rattled out of the siding. According to Tallboy's compass, it was chugging leisurely north-east.

Lying in his wire cradle, he must have suffered indescribable torments on that nightmare journey across Germany, for even when the train stopped, he dared not leave the shelter of the wagons. For nearly four hundred miles he was carried in this manner, the wire cutting into his arms and legs. But he stuck it out. To take his mind off the inverted rack on which he was stretched, he plunged into abstruse calculations in an effort to work out the distance covered at various recognizable landmarks. When the train came to a shuddering halt just outside Starogard, roughly fifty miles south of his destination, Tallboy painfully released himself, lay on the track for a time until feeling crept back into his numbed limbs, and then darted across a field towards a clump of trees. There he sank to the springy turf, luxuriating in the silence and seclusion of his green retreat. He nibbled a piece of chocolate as he waited for strength to flow back into his bruised body.

When he felt equal to the task, he struck off across country on the final leg of his journey. Pausing only to check his route with map and compass, he plunged doggedly on towards the sea.

He controlled his rate of progress so that he entered the city of Danzig in darkness. Because of the black-out, he found it difficult to work out his bearings, but after exploring a number of streets without meeting a soul, he saw at last, over and beyond a high wall, tall masts of ships cutting the night sky. He was in the dock area.

Taking advantage of his unusual height, he gripped the top of the wall, hauled himself up and over, and crouched there in the gloom, listening intently. The only sounds were the distant lapping of water, the creaking of cordage, the quick scuffle of a rat in search of food. Satisfied that the docks were deserted, Tallboy picked his way across a veritable maze of railway lines towards the edge of the quay. He had only a few more yards to go when suddenly whistles shrilled piercingly and the quay side where he stood was flooded with a blaze of light. Then followed the clatter of boots on stone, mingled shouts, more whistles. Somewhere chains jangled and machinery roared alarmingly.

Terrified by the din and blinded by the glare, Tallboy

backed away from the powerful arc lamps. Panic-stricken, he stumbled up against what appeared to be a miniature hayrick. A couple of ponies, resenting the intrusion, whinnied plaintively. He had blundered into their store of provender. Expecting at every moment a hail of bullets, he burrowed into the straw and lay still.

When the medley of noises continued and nobody came his way, Tallboy realized that the crazy activity had nothing to do with his presence in the dock area. Either a late night shift was just going on duty or a ship containing an important cargo had to be unloaded in a hurry. The reckless illumination of the quay certainly suggested emergency measures. From his vantage point, Tallboy watched the dockers troop towards one of the ships. The ungainly arm of a crane began to rotate slowly. Gearwheels meshed with a grinding clamour and giant pulley blocks thudded and rattled. In a matter of minutes the wharf had sprung to life.

In his exhausted condition Tallboy snuggled into the warmth of the hay and was soon fast asleep. He slumbered there through the rest of that night and right through the next day until dusk. When he looked about him he was relieved to see that the coast was clear. The overhead lights were out, the stevedores had vanished and the only sign of life came from one of the ponies, munching rhythmically less than a yard away. Feeling considerably refreshed after his long sleep, he struggled to his feet, crossed the railway lines and headed for the concourse of merchant ships. As he drew near he spotted a huge 'S' on the funnel of a vessel riding at anchor some little distance from the wharf side. It was a Swedish freighter.

Tallboy dived into the icy water and swam to the anchor chain. He hoisted himself up, hand over hand, and a minute later he collapsed on the iron deck. By sheer will-power he floundered towards an open hatch and tumbled into the blackness. . . .

When consciousness returned, he could feel the steady throb of the ship's engines. Above his head was a rectangle of deep blue sky and the sun was shining. He could smell the tang of the sea.

Too weak to move, he waited until he could attract the attention of one of the crew. The startled seaman lugged Tallboy to the deck and took him before the captain, who could speak good English. Tallboy told his story to the friendly Swede and shortly afterwards he was put to bed, where he received food and medical treatment. For the next forty-eight hours he lay between warm blankets, dozing for long periods, chatting occasionally with the captain and the ship's doctor, and enjoying the best of fare from the galley. He was told the freighter was bound for Stockholm.

In the meantime the captain informed the ship's owners that he had a stowaway on board. The owners, in turn, must have notified the police, for when the vessel docked, Tallboy was taken ashore and placed under arrest. At the end of his thousand-mile journey, he found himself a prisoner once again.

Eventually air transport was furnished from London to fetch Tallboy home. Usually when an escaped prisoner reached his own country, he was immediately interrogated by Intelligence, but in this case, Tallboy needed a week's convalescence before he was well enough to tell his story. For my part, as soon as I knew he was safe in an English hospital, I asked for and received permission to break the good news to the boy's father. Gleefully I hurried over to Tallboy Senior's office. I could see from his resigned expression that he thought I had come to pester him for more office furniture.

'Well, what do you want to barter this time?' he demanded.

'A body for a bottle of beer,' I replied with a grin.

He looked up at me, bewildered. 'Whose body?'

'Your son's—very much alive and kicking. He's right here in London.' I suddenly thought of something and added, 'Didn't you tell me he was engaged to be married to a girl in Edinburgh?'

Too overcome with emotion to speak, the happy father could only nod affirmatively.

'Then invite her down here next week-end,' I enthused. 'But don't say anything about the boy. We'll give her a pleasant surprise.'

And that is exactly what happened. On the following Saturday, a car drew up outside the Tallboy residence in Harrow and out stepped the young contortionist from Stuttgart, to be welcomed home by his delighted parents and the radiant Scots girl who had waited patiently and believed. . . .

After leaving the Tallboy house that same evening, I returned to London and decided to take my favourite stroll through the Green Park. It was one of those fine cloudless nights that the Luftwaffe had once found irresistible. The war was by no means over, but the skies above London held only stars and a rising moon and a promise of victory. I lifted my face to those millions of tiny lamps. Andromeda was there, and Cassiopeia dancing brightly across the Milky Way, and Ursa Major and—yes there it was, in a direct line from Merak and Dubhe—the Pole Star.

All over Europe, in hundreds of prison camps, millions of tiny needles were pointing to that star round which all the heavens seem to revolve. Heads were bent studiously over silk maps; eager fingers were squeezing dyes from fountain-pen barrels; Gigli saws were biting through the barbed wire. And from somewhere in Piccadilly a news-vendor was calling 'British Army Has Crossed the Rhine!'

Soon, I thought wistfully, somebody will be going out of business.

In the years following the conclusion of the war nearly all the details of my work and of my escape gadgets were publicized in one way or another in our own and the foreign press. Furthermore, most of the gadgets which were used in such vast numbers had been put on sale to the public.

It therefore seemed a reasonable thing that I, as the one person possessed of all the facts, should tell the whole very entertaining story. However, if one has had the privilege of serving in the Intelligence Corps one is forced by certain regulations to sign a declaration on leaving the service that no knowledge gained by virtue of such experience will be disclosed without permission. And in any case I would have welcomed advice on one or two fine points of security. Accordingly I wrote on January 4th 1950 the following letter, intending fully to discuss with the appropriate authority not only my lectures but a book upon the same subject:

The Director of Military Intelligence,
War Office,
London S.W.1.   January 4th 1950

Sir,

Later on this year I intend giving a series of lectures dealing with my experiences over many years in the motion picture business, and also other experiences including those of journalism.

I intend to incorporate in these lectures certain parts of the talks dealing with Escaping – starting before the Boer war – Mr Churchill's episode in that war – the escapes of Evans, Harrison, and others in the 1914/1918 war. I also intend to bring in certain of the published material dealing with escapes in the last conflict.

I shall be glad if you will grant me an interview on this matter as I should like to solicit your help and advice. Perhaps you will give me a date and time convenient to yourself.

Yours faithfully,

CLAYTON HUTTON

While awaiting a reply to this letter, I thought it might be a good thing to collect various newspaper cuttings and extracts in case it should be necessary to show evidence of the fact that, although most of the work I had carried out in the war was considered secret *at the time*, in view of the numerous published books and articles showing intimate details of the work there would be no chance of my publicizing anything that had not already seen the light of day.

What I collected was illuminating.

In 1943, in the middle of the war, when the word *Secret* was stamped on nearly every document handled by us, it was with considerable interest that I opened the *Sunday Pictorial* of September 12th and saw a double-column illustration under the caption 'Is THIS THEIR PASSPORT HOME?'

The illustration was taken from a German magazine and reprinted in various other foreign papers and clearly showed our first escape kit. The details of what the kit contained were accurate. Feeling somewhat annoyed, I wrote to the Editor of the *Sunday Pictorial* asking if he would tell me how it happened that he was able to publish such data; he replied to me as follows:

The information came to us in the way that all information does to newspapers, and we of course made the usual checks with the authorities.

Again, during the war *Die Wehrmacht* stated:

Each man in a U.S. Flying Fort has a compass the size
of a sixpence; money that can be used in France or
Germany; two maps printed on both sides of the
paper, and a steel file.

Immediately after the war a series of articles appeared
in the *Sunday Dispatch* from the pen of Flt Lt R. Kee.
In one dated September 30th 1945, under the title of 'The
Escape Machine', Kee went into the very greatest details
of our entire scheme. The article, one of a series, is on
pages 6 and 7 and consisted of six columns. In a separate
box at the head of the article this appeared:

This is the first full inside story of the amazing secret
society set up inside German prison camps which
completely outwitted the Nazi guards and enabled
many of our men to find their way to freedom. Flight
Lieutenant Robert Kee, of Roehampton Lane,
London, spent three years as a prisoner after being
shot down.
    He made several attempts to escape. In this, the
first instalment of a series of articles, Kee reveals the
existence of the mysterious 'Big X's', the men in
charge of the escape organizations, and of the wide,
complicated network brought into action when a
break-out was being planned.

It will be seen by this wording that the reader was
invited to a peep behind the scenes on how the escape
organization at home and in enemy camps worked. Kee
was flying in a Hampden bomber in 1942 at 800 feet
above the Friesian Islands when the machine was hit by
flak. The machine crashed on one of the islands, killing
two of the crew, but Kee and his navigator got clear, being

only slightly hurt. After a description of his descent Kee goes on to say :

> In the RAF it had been drummed into us by lectures and notices on the walls of the briefing rooms – If you are taken prisoner of war it is your duty to try to escape.

He mentions it was the *duty* of flyers to escape. This was because no orders were ever issued to troops in the first war of a similar nature. When he had recovered his senses, he says, he did not think anything of it being his duty to escape but rather 'what an impossibility to try' as he was at once surrounded by German troops with tommy guns. He did not waste much time, however, for on arrival in a transit camp he made what he called a 'pathetic attempt', and having no adequate food, maps, money, or clothing, he was of the opinion that escape was impossible. His ideas changed on his arrival in his first permanent camp :

> There I made my first contact with the highly secret escape organization run under the very noses of the Germans. The general set-up of the RAF escape organization in the camps in which I lived was complicated, even ostentatious. But it was mighty effective.
>
> An enormous 'tree', rather like a family tree, was drawn up. I remember seeing it chalked up on a classroom blackboard at a secret and well guarded meeting of the Escape Committee one hot summer afternoon. The armed German sentries were only a few hundred yards away, and in complete ignorance of what was going on.
>
> At the head of this 'tree' was 'Big X'. He had complete control of the organization.

After hearing and seeing what was then going on in the camps, Kee formed quite a different idea of his chances of escape. He then gives a concise explanation of something which was *not* taught or drummed into the boys on this side of the Channel:

> Quite a lot of our equipment for escapes was sent from England. We got it in various ways – money came to us hidden in the covers of books, maps in snakes and ladders boards, and papers and heavier items, such as hacksaw blades, came in special parcels.
>
> It is an indication of the extent to which prisoners outwitted the German security system that these special parcels were sent quite undisguised along with the thousands of other parcels in the ordinary way. All that happened was a secret warning of the despatch of such parcels from home.
>
> The British prisoners in the parcel store were given the tip to look out for special markings and the address, and as soon as it turned up in the mailbags it was quickly smuggled out of the store into the camp.

It was now clear to this young airman for the first time that some of those at home accused of being 'armchair warriors' had not been so complacent as the public imagined. In this illuminating article Kee goes on further to illustrate the help which was 'laid on':

> Later in the war some of such clothing was received from home. A brand new Royal Marine uniform arrived one day for an RAF officer who never saw it, for with the badges of rank and the buttons torn off it was an immaculate dark-blue civilian suit and went straight into the hands of the escape organization.
>
> Another RAF officer received a brand new RAF uniform which looked harmless enough except possibly for the fact that it was a slightly odd shade of blue. But when the squadron leader's stripes were

taken off the arms and a few trivial additions made, it became a faultless Luftwaffe officer's uniform.

The foregoing are only short extracts from Kee's article but as the basis of the escaping machine was now 'blown' as early as September 1945, I thought it was a good example, among several others, to take along to the War Office as they might have nothing 'on tap' when I raised the issue. To be certain of the matter I also unearthed a reply from the editor of the paper, to whom I wrote in September 1945 asking how it was that such a series of articles could appear at that time. The editor replied to me in October as follows:

> I have read with interest what you say but I think I should tell you that the article to which you refer was submitted to the Security Department for their views on it before it was published. They did not object to its form or its contents.

Thus as early after the war as 1945, a member of their own Service, with official permission, had disclosed many of the most guarded methods, including the facts that quantities of escape material was sent in 'special parcels' and that prisoners of war were warned from home of such parcels. Kee even discloses our method of sending apparently innocent suits to prisoners, which with slight alteration became German officers' uniforms.

It was therefore extraordinary for the Air Ministry to say, as they did later, 'Yes, we admit Kee gave the game away – but of course we have never admitted what he wrote was official.' What on earth would any reader think? I am quite sure he did not think thousands of parcels of escape materials were sent from Great Britain to prisoner-of-war camps without proper Government sanction.

Hearing nothing from the War Office within a week I again wrote to them on January 10th:

The Director of Military Intelligence,
War Office,
London S.W.1.   January 10th, 1950

Dear Sir,
    Further to my letter to you of the 4th instant I shall be glad to know when I may have the appointment to see you, please.

Yours faithfully,

CLAYTON HUTTON

This brought a reply by telephone to my office on the 13th from a secretary speaking for a Major of the DMI's department whom I will call Smith. He asked me if I would go and see this officer on Monday 16th. I therefore visited again, after five years, the gloomy and depressing Ministry in Whitehall, taking with me the various references. I did not have to wait very long before I was in the office of Major Smith.

I explained to this officer that I wished to have permission both to lecture in the United States and to write a book dealing with my war experiences, so that the latter could be published simultaneously in the United States with the lectures. Major Smith – a regular officer – was most sympathetic to my wishes, but pointed out he was not fully *au fait* with all that I outlined since he had only been in that branch for a short period, and he would have to put my request before the security sections dealing with such matters. I then showed Major Smith various evidence that most of the devices that I wished to write about had already seen the light of day, in the press, and some had even been sold to the public. After showing him the articles in the *Sunday Pictorial* and the *Sunday Dispatch*, I then showed him a cutting from the *Yorkshire Post* dated December 1st 1945:

ESCAPE MAP GIFTS

In a Holborn store today I came across a consignment of RAF 'escape' maps released for sale to the public. These maps, the largest a little over half a yard square, some coloured, some white, are printed mostly on an exceedingly fine silky material and fold into a very small space. They are what our airmen carried on their flights abroad so that they should know their approximate bearings should they come down.

The squares are marvels of detail and compression. Maps of Scandinavian regions, for example, carry, besides all possible place names, glossaries of the topographical terms in Norwegian, Swedish, Danish, Finnish and Russian. Now the maps will serve a peace-time purpose as mementoes, or as handkerchiefs, scarves, aprons, cushion-covers – or even maps. They cost five or six shillings and need no coupons.

I also showed him a reply from the Ministry of Supply, dated December 31st 1945, to a letter I wrote them asking how these maps came to be on sale so quickly after the war. Their reply was as follows:

With reference to the sale of 'RAF escape maps', it is *assumed* that these maps were disposed of as surplus stock in the usual manner, and it is obvious that this item of equipment is no longer 'Top Secret'. [My italics.]

This may or may not have been correct, but it was strange that among the maps put on sale were some which were very highly guarded secrets in the war, including route maps with very confidential matter on them.

This was sufficient evidence that the 'secret' maps were secret no more, by authority, but I went on to produce evidence of the compasses having being sold too. Not only had I bought many of them myself, but the *Daily Mail*, on November 10th 1946, published a picture of the compass with the following description:

> COMPASSES HIDDEN IN SWEETS
>
> Thousands of miniature 'escape' compasses, hidden in sweets in emergency food packs issued during the war to men on hazardous missions, are being recovered by the Ministry of Supply, who have so far sold 7,000.
>
> One of the compasses, taken from a sweet, is shown here – actual size. The two white dots mark the magnetic north.

As further support if necessary I also produced a statement dated January 6th 1950, that the Russians were buying large quantities of these surplus 'escape maps'. There was of course no reason why the Russians or anyone else should not buy the maps or anything else that was surplus, because in 1949, in a French antique shop, I bought one of the maps previously described as 'top secret'. It cost me four pounds, and even with a cellophane wrapping I thought it a shocking figure to charge, particularly as the cost was originally four shillings and sixpence!

I also showed Major Smith a reply to an enquiry made by the Editor of the *Daily Graphic* in 1950, asking the Air Ministry what had happened to all the redundant compasses. They replied:

Compasses were disposed of by the Ministry of

Supply at auctions and sales. A number went to Army cadet units.

Having seen this evidence in support of what I was asking, Major Smith promised he would do all he could to get me the permissions I required, and expressed his personal view that as most of the scheme had now been 'blown', there would be little trouble in my getting such permissions. I pointed out that now was a most appropriate time as in the previous month, at the request of the Ministry of Supply, I had prepared a long record of my work for submission to the Royal Commission on Awards; this had been forwarded by the Air Ministry with their blessing.

This amicable meeting ended with a request from Major Smith for a short precis of what I wanted, which he would put forward to the proper security section for consideration.

On January 19th 1950 I sent the following letter to Major Smith:

Major A. B. Smith, D.S.O.,
The DMI's Dept.,
War Office,
London S.W.1.   January 19th 1950

Dear Smith,

As I explained to you last Monday morning, I am desirous of making a series of Lectures in the United States this year, on my experiences.

I have signed a contract to do so.

It is my intention to refer to certain angles in connection with my work in the last war, but only in relation to matters that have become *public property*, and already published.

While no ban can possibly be brought to bear upon me in this direction, it will be appreciated if you will confirm to me, that no attempt will be made by the War Office to prevent me.

I suggest a letter in simple form on the lines attached would meet the case, as this does not implicate the War Office in any way. If you could let me have this at the earliest moment it will be appreciated.

Yours sincerely,

CLAYTON HUTTON

and the suggested letter I sent to the War Office for myself to hold was as follows:

Dear Clayton Hutton,

Regarding your talk with me and the outline you have given as to your lecture tour in the States and mention of your work during the war.

We cannot impose a ban upon your writing or your lecturing which might include the 'lines' you mention, neither do we wish to prevent you.

Yours etc.,

With these I sent the precis as asked for by Major Smith at our interview; this was as follows:

It is my intention during the latter part of this year to give a Lecture tour in the United States of America and in the Middle West. The Lectures will contain my experiences over some thirty years in journalism and the motion picture business.

Within those talks I intend also to give certain experiences in the first war, and also in the last.

The chief reasons why I wish to tell what was done (as far as I intend to do) in the last war are twofold: (a) the Americans copied our scheme and we started them off on it. This part I intend to do in a light and, if possible, slightly humorous way; (b) the average Englishman is treated in the United States as being a perfect fool in war matters – whereas the very reverse is the case.

M

It is not my intention or wish to blazon forth the name of the War Office or any other service. I propose to show how escaping started through the ages, bringing in the one or two chief escapes of the first war, when one was on parole, then to explain the difference in what was expected of the troops (to escape) in the last war, and how certain gadgets were given them in the last war to help them escape. I only propose to mention some of those that were *blown and had been given publicity to.*

As an example of what I mean :

1. The Service Button, with compass in same, was a universal distribution. When (after about 70,000 had been issued) it was caught, there was certain disappointment and it was thought best to discontinue it. Instead of doing that, I had a *left hand thread* put on the button, so that as the Germans examined them for some further period they continued to *tighten them up.*

2. RAF Escape Boot (Now on sale in Millett's Stores). The reason this was brought in was because, after many fellows had been shot down, the news came through that they were being impeded in their running, because the issue boot made of suede became sodden with water. I therefore evolved the leather boot made in two parts, with the penknife inside so that they could cut the top away and obtain freedom of action.

3. Ration Boxes. The difficulty of giving, in a flat ration box of such small dimensions, a ration of water. This was impossible, but was overcome by putting in the box a tube of condensed milk.

4. Fly Button Compass. To explain the very complicated problem I had to get over with the two types of buttons. The Army button was in brass (khaki). The RAF button (black) was in steel. I therefore had to marry them both, one in brass (steeled over) and vice versa.

I think this gives a rough idea of what I have in mind.

The foregoing was sufficient to put before any Committee to get sanction for lecturing or writing. I made no request at all to be given permission to lecture or write on anything that was not public property, had not already been published, or was the work of any other section.

One cannot expect large Government departments to reply to such a request the next day, particularly as what I had asked for had possibly to be checked. I was therefore very pleased to receive a letter dated January 31st 1950 from Major Smith. Evidently he had put forward my request to the proper section in a perfectly fair manner, as his letter gave me exactly what I required. He said:

> I can say that as regards your talk with me and the outline you have given me of your lecture tour, no ban will be imposed on you in this connection.

To this I replied as follows:

> Dear Smith,
> Thank you very much for your letter . . . Your generous help is much appreciated.
> Please let me know which day this week, if any, you can have lunch. Any day, except tomorrow, Tuesday.
> Yours sincerely,
> CLAYTON HUTTON

It will be observed that all correspondence and interviews had been in a most friendly spirit. There was of course no reason why they should not have been, but in view of what subsequently transpired, it is remarkable that even up to the dramatic ending of this narrative my late 'masters' at the War Office never came into the proceedings at all. Whether they were too ashamed or not I don't know, but what did happen shows what can happen to the ordinary citizen in such circumstances.

A month or two later I was in the office of a friend on one of our biggest weekly newspapers, who was talking to his printer. I mentioned that I was going to the United States later in the year to lecture on my war work, and that I also hoped to publish a book. The printer intimated that in addition to his printing he was also a director of a firm of London publishers and that he would like to have the chance of publication if his co-directors agreed. Within a few weeks the contract was signed for a book based on the material in my lecture tour, and I went to work to write the script immediately.

The book which I called *A Journey Has Been Arranged*, was completed by August. It was roughly 250 pages, containing some 60,000 words. About half the script dealt with my own work, showing many of the difficulties encountered in devising, manufacturing, and equipping our troops with the various 'aids', both at home and when they were prisoners; also the humorous side, the 'fooling' of the enemy. I also dealt with certain events in the first war: the escape of J. H. Evans, Hervey, Harrison, Bennett and others, together with extracts from speeches made by German officers in between wars. I included extracts from Geoffrey Pyke's book on the first war, and from Red Cross official international rules.

Reading the finished script through, I felt it was a simple and interesting résumé of a rather humorous side of war, giving nothing away to anyone so long after the war.

Wishing to have an expert opinion on the finished script, I could think of nobody more suited to read it than Air Marshal Sir Basil Embry. There were others whose opinion I could have sought, but Sir Basil was the first

wartime escaper to come and see me after his escape, and
when he saw the plans of our scheme in its infancy, he
became one of its strongest supporters in the RAF, who
were by the far the biggest users of the scheme. I therefore took the script to Sir Basil at his headquarters and
asked him if he would read it. Within a few days he sent
for me and told me he thought it a very interesting story
and one that should be published. He could see no security
reason why it should not be published so long after the
end of the war, when so much had already been published
on the same subject. Sir Basil further offered to write a
preface to the book. This is what he wrote:

> All aircrew of the war are indebted to Clayton
> Hutton for what he did in the cause of escape. When
> I was shot down on the 27th May 1940, I carried no
> escape aids, for the simple reason there were not any.
> Someone sitting in an office had decreed that aids
> such as compasses concealed in buttons were to be
> deprecated because if the Germans once discovered
> such deception all uniform buttons would be cut off
> and officers would look most slovenly, and, possibly,
> indecent.
>
> How I cursed that decision when I was on the run;
> I would have given my right hand for a compass,
> committed a felony for a map, and murder for a
> biscuit at the end of three days without food!
>
> It was on my return to England in August 1940
> that I first met Clayton Hutton, or 'Clutty' as he is
> known to his friends. He was sitting in his office in
> the Hotel Metropole, and I told him my story, and he
> described what he was trying to do to help aircrew
> escape. I was delighted and at once took a liking to
> him, because here was a man of action and ideas.
>
> Clutty would never allow a difficulty to stand in
> his way. Some people may think he is eccentric; I
> think he is a genius. This book tells the story of how
> many of the difficulties were overcome; some by

ingenuity, and others by sheer determination and refusal to be put off by procedure and precedent. It gives a wonderful insight into an important and thrilling activity of the war which, in my judgement, paid a dividend out of all proportion to the work and cost involved. It helped a very large number of aircrew to escape or evade, and to return to safety after having been shot down; it gave to others confidence that it would aid escape should they be shot down, and therefore helped to build morale; and it caused great trouble and vexation to the enemy and thereby struck at his morale.

After my adventure in 1940 I always flew on operational missions well prepared for an emergency; I carried a full range of escape aids, some of them duplicated. I really believe that when the end of the war came I was almost disappointed that I had not put them to the test.

BASIL EMBRY

Feeling that I had now completed a book with which my publishers would be well satisfied, and one that would be acceptable to my late masters at the War Office, I accordingly handed the finished work to the publishers, prior to giving it to the War Office for vetting. The matter seemed simple enough to me, but in fact it led to nothing but trouble and anxiety, and very nearly to tragedy.

My London publishers, who had approved the manuscript and seemed pleased with the result, showed me some circular letters sent out to all publishers from the Admiralty, War Office, Air Ministry and Press Committee. These were called 'D' notices. They were signed by one of the excellent press censors in the last war, and a highly successful man at his job.

The first notice I read, dated January 19th 1946, asked publishers to refrain from publishing certain matters relating to prisoners of war or evaders. The very points raised in this letter had, of course, been disclosed previously – with security clearance – in such articles as that by Flt Lt R. Kee on September 30th 1945 (p. 161). How such a letter came to be circulated on January 19th 1946 needs explanation – particularly as I was given permission to write and lecture on the same subjects in January 1950!

A short letter dated May 11th 1949 was also circulated, asking that no reference be published to new equipment that might be in process of being manufactured or used to help prisoners of war. This was quite a different matter, and nobody in his right senses would do such a thing; but old equipment is not new equipment. In a further letter, dated August 24 1950, publishers were again invited to refer manuscripts dealing with escaping and suchlike matters to this Committee, for 'guidance'; several books and articles had been published which had contained secret information dealing with escapers and escaping, and this had caused 'serious concern to the Fighting Service departments'. If this was so, why had no action been taken? This letter stated that the officer best qualified to vet a script was the AOC of the Air Staff (Intelligence). The circular went on : 'send the manuscript to him, either direct or through me. You will have it returned *without delay.*' Lastly, 'I can guarantee that there will be no hold-up and that no deletion will be made in the manuscript which is not regarded by Air Vice Marshal Ogilvie Forbes as essential.'

I at once asked Air Marshal Sir Basil Embry whether he would speak to a responsible officer on this Committee in an endeavour to get my script read quickly, so that I could make any changes required before I left for the United States at the end of the year. In late August he told me he had spoken to a Group Captain, who promised the manuscript immediate attention. Sure enough, early in September I was telephoned by a Squadron Leader who told me he had been deputed to see me and do all he could to assist me in the passing of the script. Progress with this officer was rapid and satisfactory. I made a few minor alterations at his request and he said he would then pass the manuscript to the Group Captain. In the middle of September the Group Captain sent for me and informed me that, though he had not had time to read the script himself, on the information given to him it presented a real difficulty to his committee. They admitted that while most of what I had written about had already been publicized before in one form or another, the complete picture I presented made the book look 'very official'.

Here, incidentally, is a golden example of the mentality of the officials vetting my manuscript. As the book dealt with escaping, I had written a long and detailed story of an escape by three officers, illustrating it with several diagrams of how they made their exit from their prison camp. During my visit to the Group Captain he confronted me with this wisdom :

'Of course, Hutton, part of our delay has been caused in checking, which has been very difficult. For example, we cannot find in our records the names of the three officers you mention, or anything about such an escape.'

'Of course, I know you can't.' I answered. 'You couldn't trace the record because, for the sake of *secrecy*, what I wrote was fiction!'

He asked me to make a series of changes and to keep in touch with a junior officer on his staff about further changes. I found the experience somewhat exasperating since it became quite clear to me from the alterations required that the officer handling the detailed vetting had no knowledge at all of the real factors involved. Nevertheless I ploughed on, and by November 10th the script was in finished form – or so I thought, until the Group Captain told me he was going to send it to the War Office for their views.

After spending much time dealing with junior officers, I seemed far from a solution, so I sought the opinion of Air Marshal Sir Basil Embry; he, feeling I was not receiving a fair hearing from the Air Ministry, wrote to the Director of Air Intelligence :

You kindly put me in touch with Group Captain Jones, who in turn handed the job to someone else who, I think, handed it to someone else. In the end I understand Clayton Hutton was given an interview, and there has been some objection to his manuscript.

I personally read through the manuscript very carefully, and although I am no expert on security, I do not believe there was anything secret which could not and, indeed, should not be published. Indeed, I agreed to write a foreword to the book, which I

would not have done if I had thought there was anything insecure in the publication.

I met Clayton Hutton a day or so ago and asked
him if the manuscript had passed through the Air
Ministry satisfactorily. He then told me it was still
being held up and that Air Ministry apparently
objected to the general theme of the book, which
seemed to me to be extraordinary and, in my judgement, without justification. It struck me that possibly
some people lower down the scale were becoming
very security-minded on a matter which I believe no
longer secret, and I would, therefore, be greatly
obliged if you would be kind enough to give this your
personal attention.

Whilst I am on this subject, I do not know what
plans the Air Ministry have in being for dealing with
escape aids, etc. in the event of another war. I don't
suppose my opinion is worth much, but I believe we
should go on some entirely new line, because if we
think we are going to get away with any of the aids
we used in the last conflict, then we are barking up
the wrong tree.

In conclusion, I would stress that I think it is of the
greatest importance that you should clear Clayton
Hutton's manuscript within the next two or three
days, or otherwise turn it down flat. If it is turned
down, however, I am going to advise him to take it
higher, because I really believe the whole of the
security line which is being adopted is absolute
nonsense.

I am sorry to trouble you, but the Air Ministry can
do themselves so much harm adopting this rather
petty approach on the question of security.

Up to that time I was under the impression that the
Committee were the beginning and the end as far as
scripts were concerned. But I was learning that the
magnificent references in the 'D' circular to speed and
personal treatment meant less than nothing. Instead I was

getting caught up in a bureaucratic labyrinth of minor
officials, none of whom, naturally, was prepared to do
anything more than raise queries. However, relying on the
promises of those who were handling the matter, I decided
to wait for the War Office views (this was some six weeks
before I was due to sail for New York). In spite of regular
enquiries on my part, no decision was forthcoming during
this period, and I left for the States in a state of uncer-
tainty and depression which was shared by my publishers.

In New York I received a letter dated January 9th. It
was from a Wing Commander (whom I had met once
during my many interviews) and contained the staggering
decision that my proposal to publish the book on the
civilian market would contravene current security policy;
the clearance I requested could not be granted. I was
warned that to ignore this decision would make me liable
to prosecution under the Official Secrets Acts.

I did the only thing possible at that distance – acknowledged its contents and asked my publishers in London to
make some enquiries on my behalf as to why the whole
book should be damned, particularly in view of the fact
that much of it had nothing directly to do with escaping.
But after four months they and their solicitors got nothing
out of the authorities except cups of tea at the Air
Ministry.

I arrived back at my London home on the afternoon of
April 30th, after a long and exhausting 20,000-mile tour
in the United States lecturing on my war work, during
which much had been going on in America at the behest
of the Air Ministry, which I knew nothing of. Waiting at
the door I found two rather sheepish-looking individuals,
who informed me that they were military officers. I asked
them inside, and the senior of the two said he had to
deliver a letter to me by hand and obtain a receipt – which

I gave to him. Whereupon they both quickly departed, looking extremely guilty and rather like a couple of naughty little boys, as if they were doing something they felt not quite right. On opening the letter, I found it was signed by an officer of whom I had never heard before, but who had apparently succeeded the Group Captain I was originally in touch with. In it I was directed to return to the Air Ministry within seven days, various articles and documents, including:

All documents procured by you (for the purpose of presenting your claim before the Royal Commission on Awards) from the contractors who had manufactured equipment for the War Office.

All manuscript, typescript and other copies of any unpublished writing or lecture relating to your service in His Majesty's Forces, and any preparatory drafts, notes, etc. for such writings or lectures which may contain information coming to you by virtue of such services.

It went on to warn me that by not conforming to this directive I would be prosecuted, and the only penalty not implied was that of death.

I could not imagine why such a letter should be sent to me, and the more I reflected on what I possessed the more did I feel certain that I had a legitimate reason for retaining everything. So I wrote a long and reasoned letter to the Secretary of State for Air on the 16th of May, the only response to which was a further letter from the Group Captain informing me that as I had not complied with his previous letter 'the appropriate steps are now being taken'. The affair was obviously fast moving to a climax, but if the Group Captain thought I was going to weaken he was mistaken.

My curiosity did not have to wait long to be satisfied. About 10.30 on the morning of June 6th, there was a ring at my door. When I opened it I saw two gentlemen leaning against the far wall. Although they were both rather tall and carried briefcases they did not give one any impression of having anything to do with the law. As I was expecting someone else I said:

'Are you from the Metropolitan Water Board?'

'No, we are two police officers,' the elder said. 'Are you Major Clayton Hutton?'

'Yes, I am – come in.'

These two officers, who always treated me with scrupulous fairness, I will refer to as Inspector Kindly and Sergeant Scribble. When I had shown them into my lounge, they told me that they had 'an unpleasant duty to perform as police officers'.

'Oh,' said I, 'and what might that be?'

As I had only previously received at the hands of the police such minor awards as summonses for simple motor car offences I was not unduly perturbed. Inspector Kindly produced from his little black case the following summons:

Christopher Clayton Hutton

Information has been laid this day by

The Director of Public Prosecution

that you within the district aforesaid, did

commit the offences set forth on Schedule attached and marked "A".

You are thereby summoned to appear before the Court of Summary Jurisdiction sitting at the Bow Street Magistrates' Court on Wednesday the 11th of

July 1951, at the hour of Two-fifteen in the afternoon to answer to the said Information.

Dated the 6th day of June 1951.

LAURENCE DUNNE

One of the Magistrates
of the Police Courts of the Metropolis

Schedule "A" attached

For that you : –

1. having in your possession or control certain sketches, models, articles and documents to which you had had access as a person who held or had held office under His Majesty, unlawfully on the 4th May 1951 in the County of London did fail to comply with a direction issued on the 26th day of April 1951 by a lawful authority, to wit the Deputy Director of Intelligence at the Air Ministry, requiring you to return the said sketches models articles and documents to the Air Ministry. (Contrary to Section 2 (1)(b) of the Official Secrets Acts 1911 and 1920).

2. having in your possession or control certain sketches models articles and documents to which you had had access as a person who held or had held office under His Majesty unlawfully on the 5th May 1951 in the County of London did retain the said sketches models articles and documents in your possession or control when you had no right to retain them or any of them. (Contrary to Section 2 (1)(b) of the Official Secrets Acts 1911 and 1920).

'I must warn you,' said Kindly, 'and make it clear to you that this summons is for a misdemeanour, and it does not say or imply that you have done anything sinister against the Crown or the Country.'

'I should jolly well think not,' I retorted. 'Now, please tell me this. Do I understand the law is that, under the

Official Secrets Act, if I or anyone else have in my possession an article that has been given to me by a properly
accredited officer of one Ministry, and if, several years
later, another Ministry, knowing that I possess this article,
and that similar articles are still in the hands of thousands
of other officers (even in the hands of the general public
since such articles had often been placed on sale) then
this second Ministry can demand the articles back from
me, under the threat of a prosecution?'

'Broadly speaking, yes,' said Kindly.

'Well, it is fantastic nonsense,' I replied, 'and it means
that I cannot defend myself. Nevertheless, let me give you
some evidence of what I mean.'

I thereupon showed him a letter from a senior officer at
the War Office.

> The War Office,
> London, W.C.2.
> 11th January 1946
>
> Dear Clutty,
> Many thanks for your letter of 9th Jan. 46. It was
> very nice seeing you again and noticing how fit you
> were looking. I am having sent off to you today a
> package containing:—
>
> 1 set 43 maps.
> 1 set 44 ,,
> 1 each Round Brass, Medium, and Midget Compasses.
> 1 Pencil Clip.
> 1 Swinger.
> 1 Each Army and RAF Fly Buttons.
> 1 RAF Button.
>
> This is the extent of our selection, as everything
> else has been disposed of.
>
> Yours ever,

This obviously shook both the detectives, and I proceeded to show them several others, including a receipt

for certain of the articles signed by the secretary to H.M. King George VI.

'Do you think the Deputy Director of Air Intelligence would care to issue a summons to this gentleman?' I asked.

'That's different,' said Kindly.

'I agree – but the fact remains that I am apparently liable to prosecution entirely at the whim of an ignorant upstart in the Air Ministry for possessing something in common with thousands of other people.'

The following day I made a long, detailed statement which was taken down in longhand by Scribble. An interesting point arose when the police began to take down my statement. On the previous evening, being under the impression I should be able to write or type my own statement, I had made rough notes on what I would say. When the police informed me that *they* would write the statement down, I said to them:

'Fair enough. Start it this way. "Many similar items, as I have shown you, which I am accused of wrongfully holding, are held by several of the highest Service officers – including King George VI. For these I have shown you the receipts. These include – "'

That was as far as I got on that line, because the police dropped their pens and said to me:

'Now, Major, really, we feel you don't want any more publicity for these people or for yourself than necessary – why bring these names in?'

To which I replied, 'Very well, then – in Court I shall bring out the names and say you "prevailed" upon me not to put them in my statement.' The police duly completed the statement, though on rather more moderate lines.

Sir Basil Embry insisted on coming to appear for me if

necessary, and we had lunch together on the day of the case. He told me, amongst other things, that he had been strongly advised by an officer not to give evidence on my behalf. Later, apparently, the officer concerned thought it might be best if the previous conversation were forgotten – 'since it might look as though we are trying to tamper with the defence's witnesses'.

'So', concluded Sir Basil, 'let us be gay and away to battle.'

It was pleasing to think I had someone in the Air Force who had faith in me.

Two days before the case was to come into Court, the two police officers suddenly arrived in my flat, very flustered.

'What's up now?' I asked them.

'Look,' one of them said. 'As we think the less publicity in this matter the better, would you mind asking Sir Basil Embry not to come to the Court in his uniform?'

I telephoned to Embry there and then, and he roared with laughter, adding, 'What rot, Clutty? Leave it to me.'

We found Scribble waiting for us at an agreed rendezvous on the 11th.

'Well,' I said, 'my witness has come as promised,' and Embry opened his small bag in which was his uniform and sword – 'just in case,' as he told the two officers.

'So I see,' said Scribble, 'but I don't think he will be requested to say anything.'

'Why not?' asked Sir Basil.

'I think you will find the case will be withdrawn,' was the reply.

With this comforting though puzzling news we arrived at the Court. The hallway was a seething mass of people and it was easy to see the majority were reporters or photographers. Not expecting such an assembly, Sir Basil and I were gripped by Kindly and rushed through a side door into the court.

'This should take about four minutes,' explained Kindly, 'and when the magistrate has finished you must dash through that door marked "Prisoners".'

'What about Sir Basil?'

'We'll bring him, too,' was the answer. 'After that we will then think how to get you both out of the court without being set on by all this mob of reporters.'

While I was thinking about this we were suddenly commanded to stand, while Sir Laurence took his seat, and I found myself in front of the dock.

A young gentleman named Mr Ian Smith then got on his feet, and addressed the magistrate:

I represent the Director of Public Prosecutions, sir. This is a case, sir, taken under the Official Secrets Act. Major Hutton was directed by an accredited officer of the Air Ministry, the Deputy Director of Air Intelligence, to return to the Air Ministry, by a certain date, various articles and documents alleged to be held by him.

This he failed or refused to do. Consequently the summons in question was issued and duly delivered on Major Hutton by appropriate officers of the court. On the offence being explained to him, Major Hutton at once offered every assistance to the officers in question, but he also made a statement. He also handed over to the officers such articles and documents as he had in his possession, explaining and showing why he held them.

Under these circumstances, therefore, the demand having been complied with, I do not wish to take up the time of the court any further, and with your permission would ask for the case to be withdrawn, sir.

There is one other point I wish to state. In this matter there is no question arising of Major Hutton, at any time, have performed anything sinister, or to the detriment of the Crown or the country, neither has anything untoward been done with any enemy power.

And with that, Mr Smith sat down.

'I'm glad to hear that, Mr Smith,' said Sir Laurence. 'Well, Major Hutton, that's it, case dismissed.'

'No sir – pardon me – withdrawn,' said Mr Smith.

'Sorry – withdrawn,' answered the magistrate.

I went with Embry through the door marked 'Prisoners', and thus ended the first defeat of the faceless men. But the Press heard nothing, other than Mr Ian Smith's short statement. This did not daunt the reporters and editors, and the National Press carried such headlines as 'HAS TO HAND OVER SECRET SKETCHES' and 'RAF GET MODELS BACK'. The facts were that all that was handed to the police was one Service button with a compass in it, and two very small silk and paper maps, which were returned to me in due course! But it took me many months to get back my manuscript from the Air Ministry, the excuse given finally being that they thought it would not be required by me any further 'in view of the circumstances'. One theory of mine – with some supporting evidence – was that they had photostatted the manuscript, though even the Air Ministry could not take several months to accomplish that simple feat.

The reader may, by this time, be getting the impression that I am over-drawing the picture, or perhaps being a little unfair because of a natural prejudice. This is not so, and I am quite aware that the Ministries have not an undue proportion of imbeciles or villains in their employ. What I do say is that the Service machines are so huge and so full of obscure officials – few ever assuming the responsibility of saying 'yes', particularly in wartime – that a vast number of minor decisions are never taken except in a negative or delaying sense. The thought motivating the entire lives of their officials is rather naturally 'I must *never* err on the side of generosity: always I must be *safe*.' The result is that as these nonentities know very little about the larger issues involved they are constantly saying 'No' in matters about which, if handled by someone really well informed, the answer would be 'Yes, of course'.

One other unpleasant feature of dealing with these Ministries is the lack of continuity of personnel, with resulting confusion to all concerned – particularly the longsuffering outsider. A priceless example of this in my history has nothing to do with escaping. Between the two World Wars I made many applications to receive my first War medals and failed dismally. During the second War I even made eight unsuccessful applications. Nobody seemed to know where to look or where to find them. Then, when I was feeling particularly annoyed with all the Service Ministries in 1950 I decided on the one course of action that seemes invariably to produce results – I sent a telegram to the War Office saying that unless I had my First War medals within seven days I would have the matter raised in the House. The very next day my telephone rang. An officer at the *Air Ministry* told me, in something of a pother, that the medals had been found there, where they had been since the end of World War I. They arrived forthwith! – and the *Evening Standard* ran a headline: 'HIS MEDALS CAME BY TAXI'!

It is hardly surprising that for the time being I gave up
any idea of publishing my story, for in addition to placing
an inexplicable ban on the complete manuscript in this
country the Air Ministry continued their machinations in
America, where Appleton-Century-Crofts had contracted
to publish the book*. The following letter was sent to Mrs
Virginia B. Carrick of this publishing house on 28th May
1951 (the italics are mine):

Dear Mrs Carrick,
    Reference is made to our letter dated 11th April
1951 wherein it was stated that this office was awaiting an opinion from the Department of Justice as to
whether or not publication of the manuscript 'An
Escape Has Been Arranged' by British Major C.
Clayton Hutton would be in violation of United
States Federal Laws.
    The Department of Justice has advised that on the
basis of the information furnished, *it could not
undertake at this time to determine* that publication
of the manuscript would furnish appropriate basis for
federal action; notwithstanding the fact that the
manuscript does contain information which retains
security classification. This opinion is predicated on
the fact that the information is within the public
domain by virtue of prior disclosure during Major
Hutton's lectures. Accordingly, no legal action is
anticipated by the Department of Justice at this time
to preclude publication of the manuscript.
    It is the opinion of the Department of the Air
Force, independent of any statutory provisions, that
publication of this manuscript would be prejudicial
to the interests and prestige of the United States

*Appleton-Century-Crofts did not proceed with publication.

Government. In this regard, the British authorities have advised that for security reasons, they have stopped the publication of this manuscript. They have also requested the assistance of the United States Air Force in preventing the publication in the United States of the manuscript under discussion.

In light of the above, the Department of the Air Force *requests* that your company refrain from publishing Major Hutton's manuscript 'An Escape Has Been Arranged'.

Sincerely,

WILLIAM M. TURNER
Colonel, U.S. Air Force

This means that though the American authorities could not find that the book infringed any federal law they felt they must appeal to the publishers not to proceed with publication in the light of the British authorities' attitude.

Nor was this all, for after a second lecture tour in America in 1953 I wished to obtain a re-entry permit so that I could return to conclude some business affairs entirely unconnected with this book. To my surprise there arose a number of delays and difficulties which actually lasted *three years*, before I received the following letter:

American Embassy,
25 Grosvenor Square,
London W.1.
August 14th, 1956.

Sir,

Reference is made to previous correspondence regarding your application for an immigrant visa.

The Embassy is pleased to inform you that after careful review of the circumstances of your case it has been determined that you are *not ineligible* to receive a visa under under the provisions of Sections 212(a) and (29) of the Immigration and Nationality

Act. We are therefore prepared to give renewed consideration to any application for a visa which you
may wish to make.

Very truly yours,

N. NEDDEN
American Consul

The only possible explanation of this delay was that
the British authorities had so blackened my name that I
had been in some peculiar way regarded as an undesirable
person to visit the USA.

In the meantime, however, I had been working on a
new version of my story and in August 1954 entered into
a contract with a new publisher for its publication. At
the publisher's suggestion I agreed to have the assistance
of Mr Charles Connell in preparing the final manuscript
for press. I therefore left him alone with the problem of
rewriting and revision for several months, but began to
get somewhat concerned when the middle of 1955 had
been reached without my being shown the finished draft.
On being assured all was going well I sat back and waited.

About 8.30 on the night of 25th November, 1955 I was
telephoned by the Military Correspondent of the *Daily
Express*, Hugh Pond. He said he had just received a copy
of a new book entitled *The Hidden Catch*, written by
Charles Connell, but which he recognized as the story of
my work at the War Office.

Hugh Pond kindly rushed to my home in his car and
showed me the book. After considering the next step we
went to the *Daily Express* with the intention of doing an
article for the next morning's issue. But, as might be
expected, no one at the Air Ministry could be found who
would discuss the affair and the Editor took the correct
view that it was best to wait until we knew what had
happened, which was as follows.

Connell, whom I have always found to be a delightful fellow, had been persuaded by the publishers that it would be wiser to let them have the manuscript direct. This they then decided to submit to the Air Ministry for clearance, and once again I was thus in their grip (without knowing it!)

On this occasion they set about slicing the story to pieces with such gusto that it was rapidly reduced from 60,000 words to a pathetic 20,000-odd. More extraordinary still, it was arranged that my name was not to be mentioned and, to make sure of this, I was to be identified only as a mysterious "Mr X". Lastly they demanded that the following paragraph be inserted:

> For all dubious decisions and unorthodox behaviour I accept full responsibility. My tale, therefore, concerns my activities only, and not those of any organized group, and I take this opportunity, right at the outset, of dissociating myself completely from all Service machinery.

There was only one solution to this – and on December 20th, before Mr Justice Danckwerts in the High Court, I sought an injunction to prevent the sale of the book. The court was packed, the air was electric – and I smelt a rat. I was right – the Air Ministry were at it again! My Counsel began to outline the case, but before he could read my affidavit he was stopped in his tracks by Mr Neville Faulks, Counsel for the Air Ministry and the publishers. He notified the judge that – under the Official Secrets Act – the Air Ministry objected to having my story read. The judge thereupon suggested that the two Counsel should have a chat, which they proceeded to do in my presence. To my astonishment Mr Faulks said that he had only been instructed the previous night, and frankly knew very little about the case. The sequel to this was that permission was sought – and granted – for an adjournment.

During the adjournment the following demands of mine were met: that the copyright of the book was to be mine and not Connell's, that my name was to go on all future books, and that to this end all unsold stock of the existing edition was to be withdrawn from sale. Furthermore the withdrawal of the passage which I naturally regarded as libellous was agreed to by Mr Faulks. An order was made by Mr Justice Upjohn in the High Court on 13th January, 1956 that these terms had been agreed. But the fact remained that the sale of my book (such as it was) was damaged beyond repair and I could thus only record a second Pyrrhic victory over the Air Ministry.

It only remains for me to record the result of my endeavours to ascertain who it was at the Air Ministry that had required the infamous insertion 'dissociating myself from all Service machinery'. Were it not for the cruelty of the libel this would of course have been comic – for, as any reader must have deduced, where were all the vast sums of money coming from that were necessary for my projects? And how, in wartime, could I possibly have accomplished all I did without full official support?

Yet this ludicrous insertion fascinated me and I tried to get to the bottom of it. First of all I wrote to the Chief Censor, asking who had passed the final text. He replied that 'The Air Ministry dealt with *The Hidden Catch* as now published and passed it for publication'. I then wrote to the Under Secretary of State for Air asking who had passed it for publication. Back came the fantastic answer: 'There is no record of a book with the above title having been submitted by a serving member of the Royal Air Force for clearance.' This sent my blood pressure up several points and being, as I have indicated, a firm believer in the use of telegrams with the Service Ministries, I sent the following broadside at 9.30 a.m. on 22nd December, 1956:

> AIR MINISTRY, WHITEHALL LONDON S.W. YOUR LETTER TWENTIETH 9374 STOP YOU MUST ALL BE STARK MAD AT THE AIR MINISTRY OF COURSE THE SCRIPT WAS SUBMITTED AND OFFICIALLY PASSED I POSSESS THE AUTHORITY WHAT I DEMAND TO KNOW IS WHICH OFFICER PASSED IT AND HIS NAME.
>
> CLAYTON HUTTON

As I imagined, this produced an immediate effect and in the afternoon I was telephoned and invited to meet a Wing Commander X who had dealt with the manuscript. After seeing my solicitor first I appeared at the new Air Ministry headquarters in Whitehall in the afternoon. At the head of the escalator, more imposing than anything London Transport has yet devised, I was pounced upon by the Wing Commander, steered into his office, and introduced to the other occupant, a handlebar-moustached Squadron Leader whose only words during the next one and a half hours were 'How do you do?' and 'Good Afternoon'.

The Wing Commander began with the obvious intention of pouring oil on troubled waters, apologizing for this and that and referring to the general confusion caused by Connell's part in the MS. However, what I had principally come for was to probe the matter of the extraordinary paragraph painting me as an irresponsible civilian who somehow was allowed to go round the country spending a fortune on ideas and gadgets for helping the Armed Forces to escape from prisoner-of-war camps.

To my astonishment, the Wing Commander cheerfully admitted that he had helped to draft the paragraph. He then proceeded to give me a long lecture on the powers the Services possessed under the Official Secrets Act, which included one passage to the effect that, in the interests of the Crown, they could say absolutely anything they liked, true or untrue, regardless of the damage they might do to someone like myself. And when I found that he was not prepared to compromise on that I did indeed feel I had come to the end of this particular road. I thanked him for a most illuminating experience, and bade good afternoon to him and his very quiet associate.

Postcript

You may think that, having forced my way at last through the bureaucratic labyrinth, I am biased against various Air Ministry and War Office officials. This is not so. I do feel however, that in this modern age of speed the present Services set-up is totally unable to provide the drive and energy needed in the advancement, testing and adoption of new ideas. Timid self-preservation prevents many officers and others from accepting responsibility through one thing – fear of 'having a go' and bringing down the wrath of their seniors upon their heads.

If this story does nothing else I hope it may prevent any part of the past scheme being used again should this country ever be drawn into another conflict.

Fortunately our Services, in time of war, always produce the right brain for the job eventually. No doubt this will happen again, and the fuddy-duddies with the lance-spear-and-bayonet minds who always seem to be in control when – but thank goodness only when – a war begins, will be routed once more. For lives are more important than **honours.**